Lake Superior, Wow!

Marlor Press, Inc.

LAKE SUPERIOR, WOW!

ISBN 0-943400-73-2
First Edition
Manufactured in the United States of America
Distributed to the book trade by Contemporary Books, Chicago, Ill.
and in Canada by Fitzhenry & Whiteside, Ontario.

Cover design by Georgene Sainati   Cover art by Jane Gibout

Disclaimer: The author and the publisher have made best efforts prior to publication to report current data. However, prices, times, facilities and services are subject to change at any time. This book is intended only as a general guide; parents should use their own judgments and discretion on specific events and attractions. In any event, the author and Marlor Press Inc. are not responsible for price changes, schedules, services, availabilities, facilities, agreements, damages or loss or injury of any kind.

MARLOR PRESS, INC.
4304 Brigadoon Drive, Saint Paul, Minnesota   55126

CONTENTS

Duluth Waterfront

Superior Waterfront

Duluth Attractions

Duluth Events

Superior Attractions & Events

Carlton

The North Shore

Acknowledgements

The author would like to acknowledge the assistance of his research staff, Jane, Jonathan & Elliot, and the efforts of Lillian Kulenkamp whose help in researching the North Shore and editing were greatly appreciated.

I would also like to acknowledge the contributions of Christine Osthus, Mike Winer, Emmily Kulenkamp, Charlie Cree, Todd Johnson, Ted Allison and Tom Dickson, who contributed to the fishing section.

Maps

Special Illustrations

Map of Lake Superior

Circled area shows Duluth, Superior and the North Shore shown on the larger map (above)

HOW TO HAVE FUN WITH THIS BOOK

Congratulations! You are about to have a lot of fun in Duluth, Superior, and Minnesota's North Shore. There are many things to see and to do in this area's big waters, open skies, and deep woods.

Duluth is the farthest inland port in America for ocean-going ships. Lake Superior is the largest freshwater lake in the world.

You'll find a park alongside a canal where giant ships pass so close it seems you can almost reach out to touch them. There's a special boardwalk along the lake you where you can walk or skate. And there's a huge bridge—the largest aerial lift bridge in the world—that rises to let ships through.

Lake Superior, Wow! is arranged for handy use. Probably, the first thing you'll want to see is the waterfront, so that's right up front. You'll find, first of all, the Duluth Waterfront. It's followed by the Superior Waterfront. Here you can find out about the ore boat tour, the Park Point beaches, or a museum on board an old boat.

Later in the book you'll find attractions throughout the rest of Duluth and Superior. You can find out where to go to climb onto antique trains, find a zoo where you can pet animals, or search for agates. There are several special train rides you can take, too.

The book also tells you about the North Shore and what you can see and do there.

A special map begins each section. That's so you can locate the place or the event you want to go to.

Each attraction tells where it is located, when it is open, and cost, if any. Most are either free or low in cost.

You will find that Lake Superior can be a lot of fun. In the skies, the gulls fly in circles. There's the scent of fresh water in the air.

And everywhere you will find interesting things to see and do. This book is your guide.

In the back, you will find a planning guide of how to get the most out of your visit to Duluth and Superior if you only have a short time. There's also a place for you to write down what you want to see and do.

ON THE WATERFRONT

☆ DULUTH AREA

☆ SUPERIOR AREA

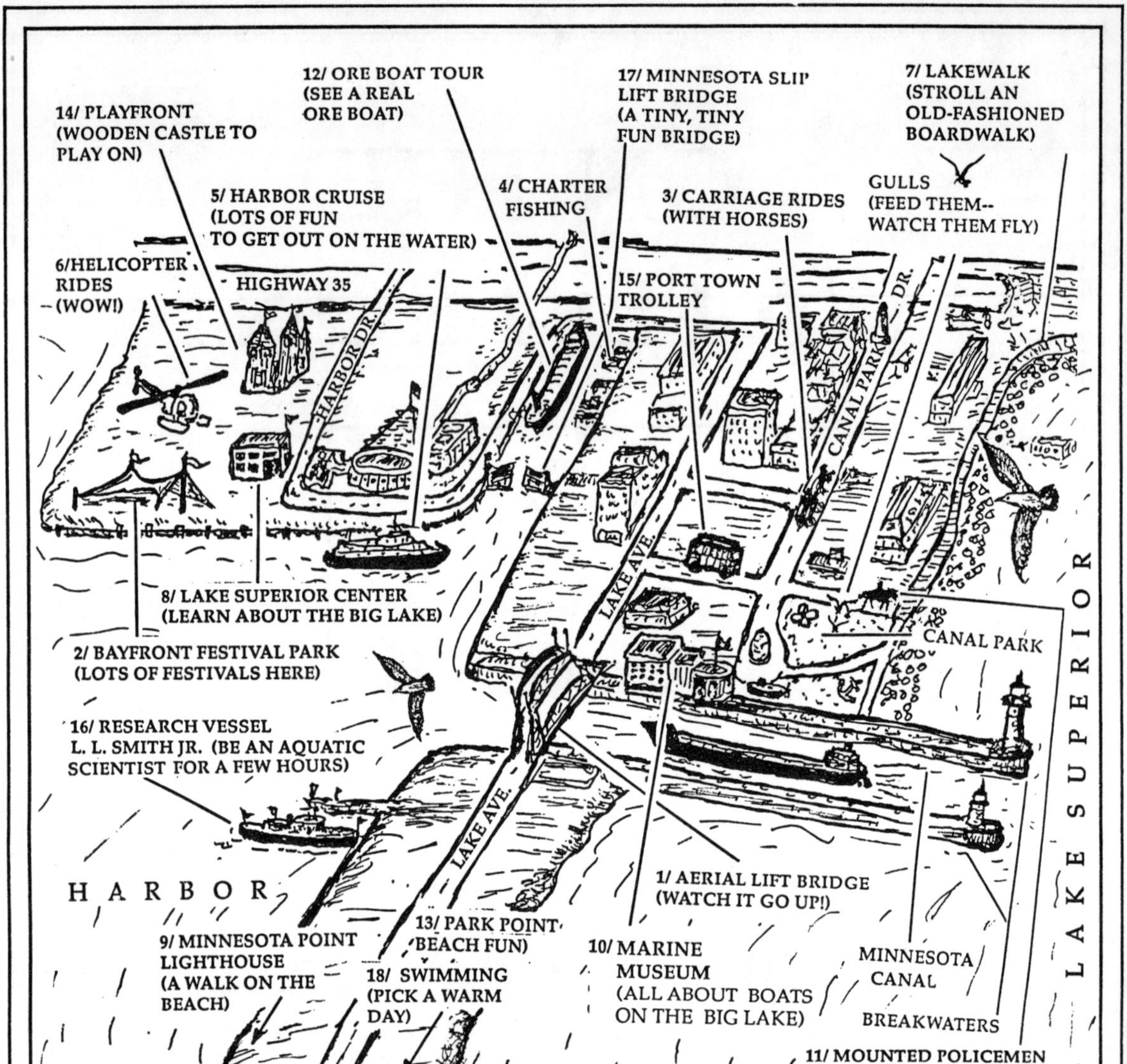

WATERFRONT ATTRACTIONS

DULUTH AREA

Waterfront attractions

1/ Aerial Lift Bridge

Take Lake Avenue south to the waterfront. Free

Duluth's best-known landmark is its Aerial Lift Bridge. Built in 1929, this is the largest and fastest lift bridge in the world. It rises to 138 feet in 55 seconds. The bridge links Duluth with Minnesota Park Point.

When it opens, you can see ocean-going freighters and Great Lakes ore boats sailing underneath. A good view is from Canal Park, next to the Marine Museum. Each time a boat comes, there'll be a loud signal---and up will go the giant bridge.

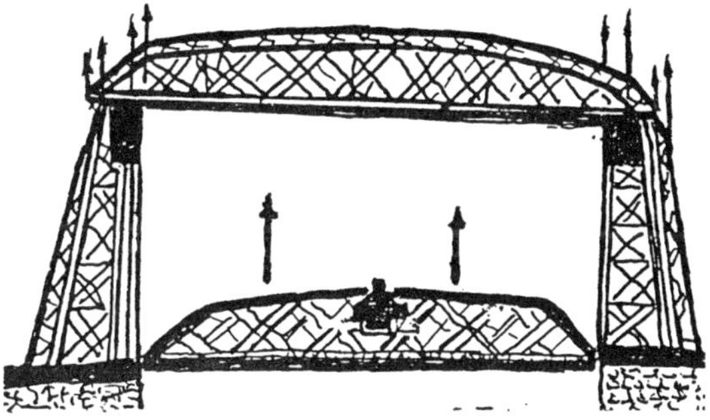

UP! The big bridge begins to rise...

AND UP! Now it's halfway up...

HIGHEST! Giant ships can pass underneath!

2/ Bayfront Festival Park

On the waterfront, near Harbor Drive. Free

This waterfront park, with the bright yellow awning, is a good place to stretch your legs and look over the magnificent harbor. Here you can usually see a number of ships at anchor or entering or leaving. The park is home for a number of events each year, including the Bayfront Blues Festival, arts and craft shows, ethnic festivals, and musical events.

Waterfront festivals are held under the bright yellow awning.

3/ Carriage Rides

Hail a horse drawn carriage on the waterfront near Canal Park. Or call Top Hat Carriage Service, (715) 399-2436. About $20 for a ride of 15 to 20 minutes.

Look what's clopping down the street. It's a brightly-painted old-fashioned carriage pulled by a horse.

The driver will pick you up in Canal Park. The ride takes you through the downtown and Canal Park area. The ride varies in cost with the length. Allow from 15 minutes to 1 hour.

4/ Charter fishing

Waterfront near the S.S. Irwin, to the east of the Duluth Entertainment Convention Center. Visit the fleet in their docks. Or call Duluth Tourist Information 800-4 DULUTH for the list of charter captains. Expensive. Half and full-day charters available.

There's a variety of fishing boats available for charter that will take kids and their families dashing out into the cold waters of Lake Superior. If you want a thrill you will talk about for years, this could be it: going out on a professional fishing boat to fish the big waters.

It's not only sport, but a great look at the world's largest freshwater lake. The boats usually provide the necessary fishing equipment.

A caution: take warm clothing because it can be chilly out on the lake. Try to pick good weather.

5/ Harbor Cruise

Vista Fleet, dock on Harbor Dr., near the Duluth Entertainment & Convention Center, May 15 to mid-October. Departs in summer schedule every 2 hours 9:30 A.M. to 7:30 P.M. daily. Adults $7.50, children 3 to 11 $3.50, free under 3. (218) 722-1728.

Children can enjoy the harbor on board the *Vista Queen*, the *Vista King*, or the *Vista Star*. The cruises on the modern steel vessels last about two hours, are narrated, and give a close-up look at lake freighters, grain elevators, the world's largest coal docks, ocean-going ships, and giant ore docks. If the weather is OK, the boats sail under the Aerial Lift Bridge into Lake Superior. The *Vista Star* has lunch, dinner and moonlight cruises. A field trip study guide is available for groups. The harbor cruises are an adventure for most children and highly recommended.

The *Vista Star* with the Duluth Aerial Lift Bridge in the background

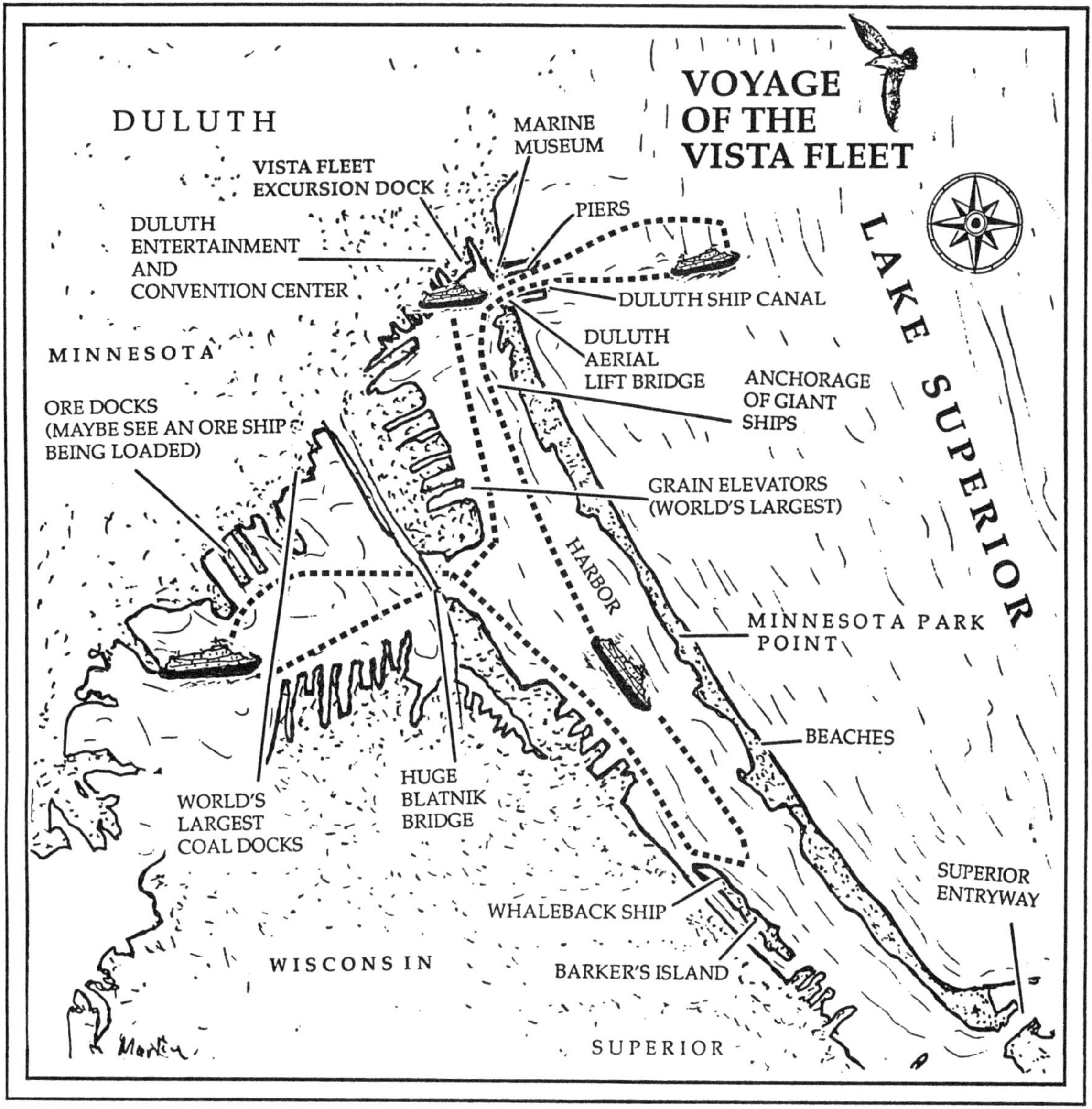
VOYAGE
OF THE
VISTA FLEET
DULUTH
MARINE
MUSEUM
VISTA FLEET
EXCURSION DOCK
PIERS
DULUTH
ENTERTAINMENT
AND
CONVENTION CENTER
DULUTH SHIP CANAL
LAKE SUPERIOR
MINNESOTA
DULUTH
AERIAL
LIFT BRIDGE
ANCHORAGE
OF GIANT
SHIPS
ORE DOCKS
(MAYBE SEE AN ORE SHIP
BEING LOADED)
GRAIN ELEVATORS
(WORLD'S LARGEST)
HARBOR
MINNESOTA PARK
POINT
BEACHES
HUGE
BLATNIK
BRIDGE
WORLD'S
LARGEST
COAL DOCKS
SUPERIOR
ENTRYWAY
WHALEBACK SHIP
WISCONSIN
BARKER'S ISLAND
SUPERIOR

6/ Helicopter Rides

Bayfront Festival Park across from the Duluth Entertainment and Convention Center (DECC).
(218) 727-6326 or (218) 879-0056
Memorial Day through Labor Day and weekends in September.
Monday-Saturday 10 a.m. to 8 p.m.
Sunday Noon to 8 p.m.
***Harbor Flight*, $10 for 3 minutes; *Over the Loop*, $15 for a 4-5 minute flight over Lake Superior; *Glensheen*, $20 for 7-8 minutes over the shore to Glensheen & back; *Lester River*, $30 for 11+ minutes to Lester River & back**

This is a chance to get a bird's eye view of Duluth and Lake Superior and to experience what some kids say is "the best roller coaster theme-park ride ever." If you haven't been in a helicopter, this is a chance to feel the sensation. Most people get a terrific charge out of being up in a "chopper." The flights are subject to favorable weather. The helicopter has a capacity of one pilot and two passengers. The handicapped can be accommodated. Bring a camera.

7/ Lakewalk

Located along the waterfront.
Walkway begins at Canal Park.
Free

An old-fashioned lighted boardwalk path runs from Canal Park, near the Aerial Lift bridge, for about a mile directly beside Lake Superior. It's a great place to stroll and look out at the big lake. A side path allows kids to roller skate or ride bikes.

Markers at overlooks give you some of the history of the lake and point out areas of interest (such as where sunken ships lie). There's a mosaic-tiled wall depicting the history of the Great Lakes. The Vietnam Veteran's Memorial is on the northern end of the walk.

The walk gives everyone an appreciation of the beauty and the awesomeness of Lake Superior. As you walk, you'll undoubtedly see sailboats and ships plying the big lake's chill waters.

LAKEWALK (above) is an old-fashioned boardwalk that parallels the Lake Superior Shoreline (see map, right).

8/ Lake Superior Center

On Harbor Drive near the waterfront.
(218) 720-3033
Open 11 a.m. to 5 p.m., Wednesday through Sunday; closed Monday and Tuesday. Open Memorial Day through Labor Day. Free

This center is devoted to understanding of Lake Superior, the world's largest freshwater lake. There's a space view of Lake Superior in a color mural, taken from 400 miles up, and a colorful multi-media program about the lake. There are also other exhibits.

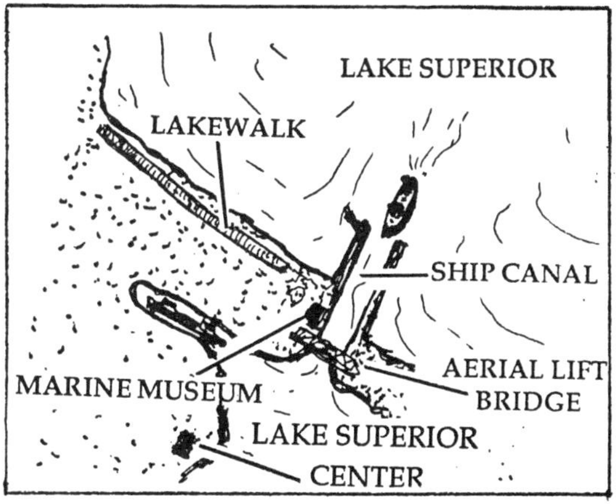

9/ Minnesota Point Lighthouse

At the far eastern end of Minnesota Point. Free

You can see the ruins of a lighthouse built in 1858. To reach it, cross the Aerial Lift Bridge and drive as far out on the Minnesota Point as you can go. The road ends at the airport. It's about a two-mile walk across sand beaches to reach the lighthouse ruins. You walk past the remnants of an old sunken ship, the *U.S.S. Essex*. The sandy beach is great fun to walk on but it can make it hard going for young children. Watch out for the poison ivy. Continue on the nature trail to see the Superior ship entry.

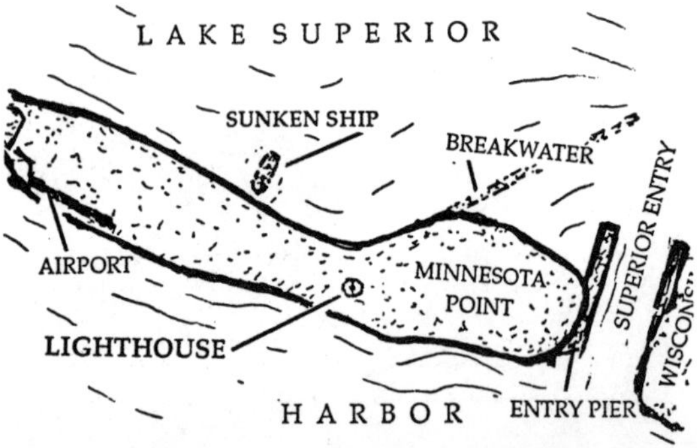

10/ Marine Museum and Canal Park

**Free. Open year round.
Boat watchers hotline, 24-hour information on arrivals and departures of vessels (218) 722-6489
Museum information (218) 727-2497.
Open every day during shipping season and three-day weekends (Friday-Sunday) during non-shipping/ winter months. Hours vary. The minimum is 10 a.m. to 4:30 p.m. Longer in mid-summer.**

The Corps of Engineers Marine Museum contains artifacts and ex-

Gulls! Gulls! Gulls! Feed them and watch the fun

The lawn in front of the Marine Museum and Canal Park is also home for lots of gulls. Kids like to toss small bread chunks up and watch the gulls fly by and snatch it in mid-air. Hint: bring old bread to toss to the gulls. Remember that the gulls are wild creatures and kids should never hold up food for them to take, play with them, or get too close. Ring-billed gulls are most commonly seen in summer. The larger Herring gulls are farther north.

Gulls fly into the air as kids toss them bread crumbs. In the background is the lighthouse at the end of the North Pier.

11/ Mounted Policemen

May to October. Free.

You can see policemen riding their horses along the waterfront. The best place to find them is usually near Canal Park. Take the camera.

12/ Ore Boat Tour

S.S. William A. Irvin
Waterfront. Berthed near Lake Ave.
Daily 10 a.m. to 4 p.m. May 1 to May 21; 10 a.m. to 6 p.m. to June 14; 9 a.m. to 6 p.m. to Sept. 5; then 10 a.m. to 4 p.m. to October 17. Halloween open evenings for special haunted tour, "Ship of Ghouls."
Adults $5 for 60-minute regular tour, $7 for hardhat tour; Children 3 - 11, $3 for regular tour, $4 for hardhat tour. No one under 8 admitted on hardhat tour. Children under 3, free.
Free parking (218) 722-7876

The flagship of U.S. Steel's Great Lakes fleet, the "Pride of the Silver Stackers," the *S.S. William A. Irvin* gives you a close-up look at past era of Great Lakes' shipping. The *Irvin* operated on the Great Lakes for 40 years and retired in 1978. The 610-foot laker was built to have important guests on board as well as to ship ore. You get to go from the crew's quarters aft to the wheelhouse up near the bow. This may be the biggest boat you'll ever see close up. There is a good deal of stair climbing.

The WILLIAM A. IRVIN

Color this Great Lakes ore carrier, now a floating museum

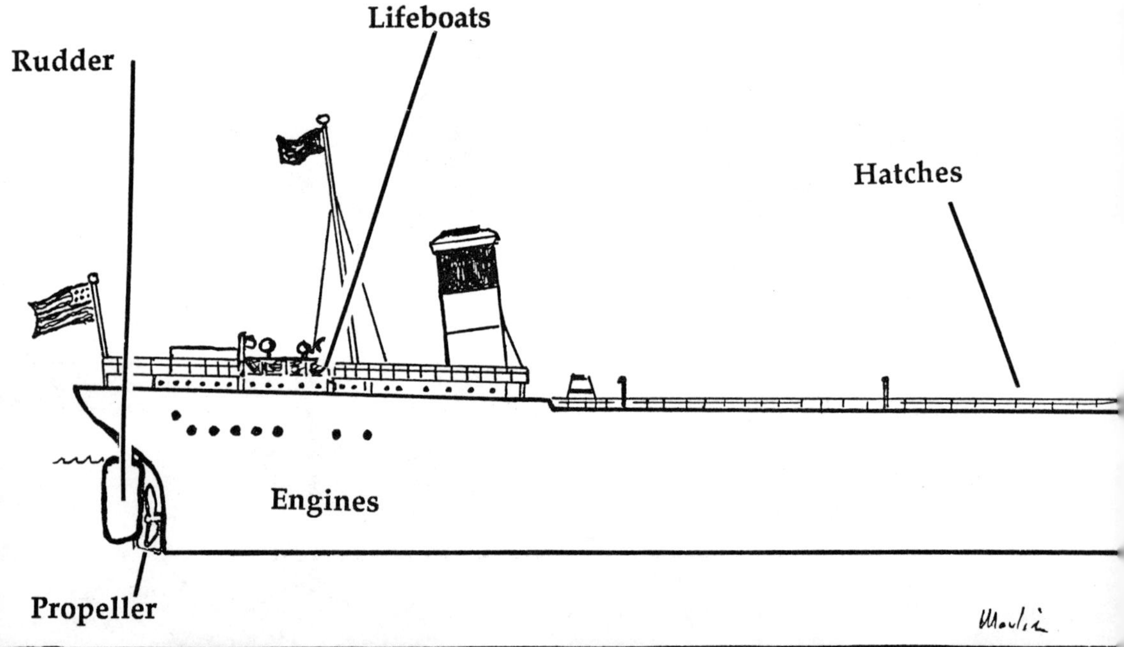

The *S.S. William A. Irvin* could carry 14,000 tons of iron ore. Her propeller is 15 feet, six inches in diameter and made of bronze. Her two steam turbines could generate 2,000 horsepower each. She moved at a speed, fully loaded, of nearly 11 m.p.h., and burned 2,400 pounds of coal an hour. Her bow anchors each weighed nearly 8,000 pounds each. It took a crew of 36 to run this big ship.

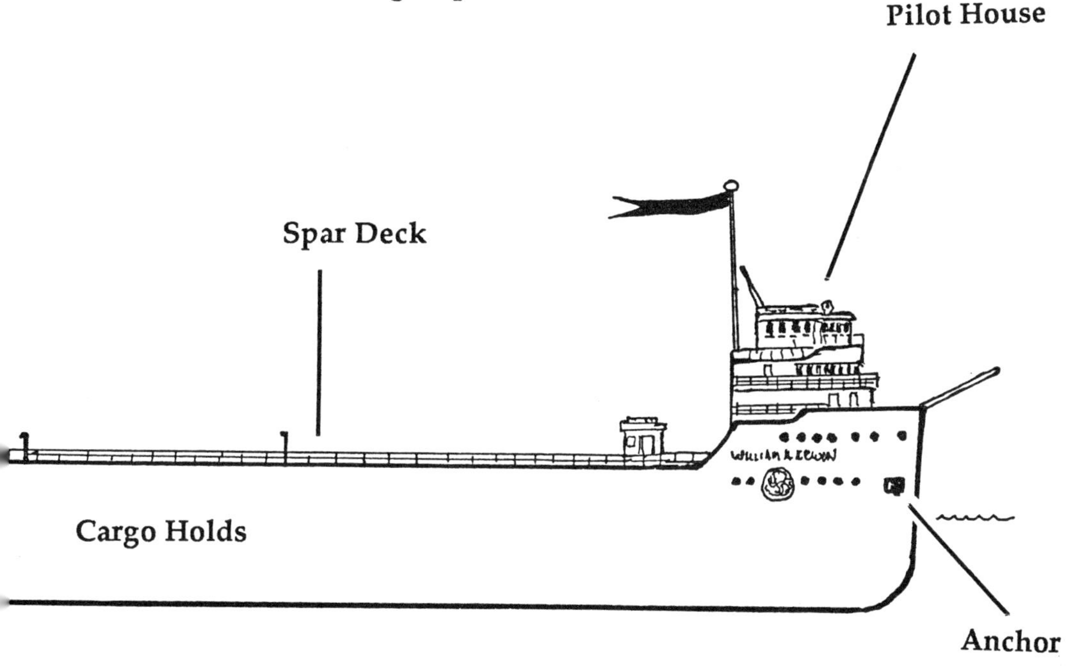

13/ Park Point Beaches

End of Park Point. Free

Cross the Aerial Lift Bridge and drive down the Minnesota Point to the parking lot just west of the airport. Don't worry about which road to take. There is actually only one big road running the length of the Point.

Walk over the sand dunes. And there you are: miles of sandy beach.

Wading and swimming are fun on a warm day. This is the world's largest freshwater sand bar, nine miles long. It is also a good place to view migrating birds, look at boats and collect driftwood. There is enough sand here for the world's largest sand castle. Bring shovels and buckets.

The Park Point Recreation Area has a beach house with rest rooms and concession stands.

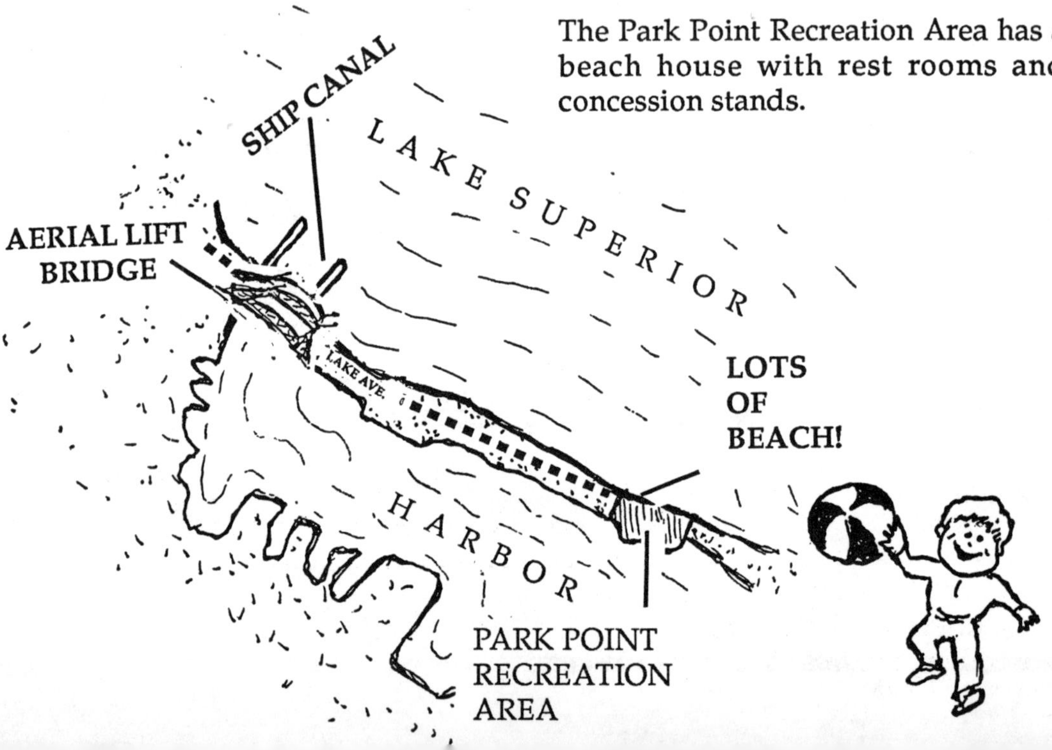

14/ Playfront Park

Bayfront Festival Park.
Free

Here is a spectacular wooden castle and a dragon—the outdoor climbing playground you dreamed about. Great fun. If you have been driving for several hours and need to get out to burn off energy, this is a good place to do it. Plan for up to an hour of climbing around.

15/ Port Town Trolley

Downtown and the waterfront.
The route goes from Fitgers, Holiday Inn, the Radisson, the Depot, Playfront park, Canal Park, the Marine Museum, and the Park Inn. ou can board at any stop along the route
. (218) 722-7283
Memorial Day through Labor Day.
11:10 p.m. to 6:48 p.m.
Adults 50 cents and children 25 cents per ride, under 3 free.
Day pass, ride all you want for $1.

This is an old-fashioned, bell clanging trolley that goes through downtown and the harbor area. The kids like the clanging of the bell. It is a different ride from a bus or a train.

The full loop takes about half hour. This can be a fun way to get around to see the city.

16/ Research Vessel L.L. Smith Jr.

Based in the Duluth Superior Harbor
Docked on Park Point near the Coast Guard Station
May through October
3-hour tours, $12 adults, $7.50 children 10 and under
Information (715) 394-8315

The *L. L. Smith* is a 58-foot steel tug equipped with research equipment. It is operated by the University of Wisconsin, Superior. The public three-hour ecology cruises are designed to let kids get an idea of what aquatic scientists do. The cruise has short lectures and slide shows on the way to the aquatic sites.

Samples from the lake bottom are collected and then students examine them under microscopes in the ship's lab. This is an interesting and informative way to learn more about Lake Superior.

It is wise to make reservations well in advance. The vessel charters out for group workshops and operates from various locations during the sailing season.

17/ Minnesota Slip Lift Bridge

Free.
Between the Duluth-Superior excursion boat dock and the waterfront plaza marina.

This is a pedestrian lift footbridge that fascinates kids (of all ages) when it goes up and down. While in the Canal Park area, be sure to walk across the bridge. You can get a fine view of the water and the boats moored nearby. A fun five minutes.

18/ Swimming

Park Point Recreation Area
Pick a warm day. Free

Go out on a very warm day with very little breeze. That's so that the sun can warm the water near the shore. You'll find that even Superior's chilly waters warm up to nearly 70 to 80 degrees on these days.

A good place to swim in Lake Superior is the beach at Park Point Recreation Area. It is at the end of Park Point. This area has lifeguards from June to late August. It has a beach house, concession stands and rest rooms.

In addition to swimming, you can picnic here and play games in the sand. Parking is free in the parking area.

If Lake Superior's water is too cold for swimming, you can have a good time wading or playing on the beach. This is one of the most terrific beaches around. You can also collect drift wood.

You can take a hike out toward the end of Minnesota Point to see the remnants of an old U.S. Navy vessel, the *U.S.S. Essex*. You can also see the 1858 Superior Entry Lighthouse. There is also a nature walk and you can do some bird watching.

Local swimmers also swim in the Lester River. This local swimming hole is near the railroad bridge which crosses the river. The swimming beach can be accessed through Lester Park. In any event, be very careful in the water and don't venture out unless you can swim well. Have adult friends watching after you.

Types of Boats

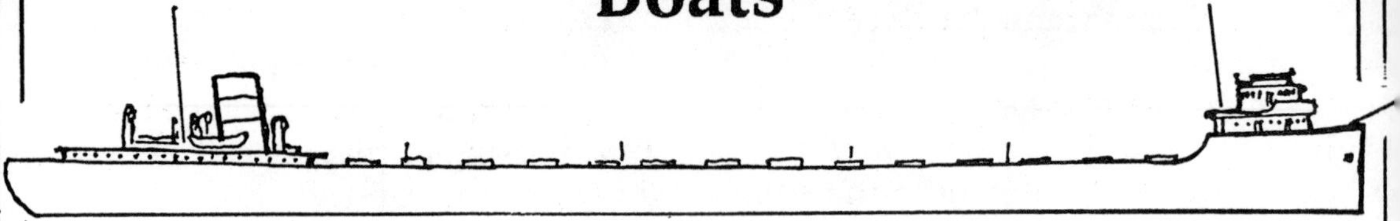

Ore boat. There is a long space on deck where the ore hatches are.

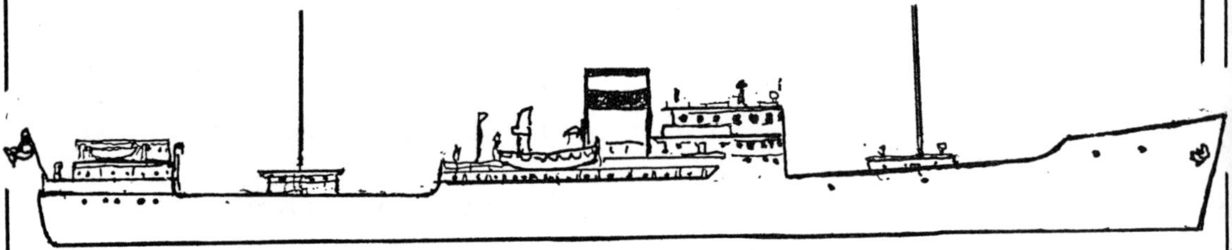

Ocean-going ship. This one crosses the seas to come to Superior.

Marlin

Sailboat. See its tall mast and sails.

Superior, Wisconsin

Waterfront Attractions

1/ Barkers Island

Hwy 2 and 53, Superior
(715) 392-7131 or (800) 826-7010
Many activities, a focal point of recreation in Superior. Free

You can see lots of sailboats here and in the harbor. Barkers Island has a 420-slip marina and is one of the largest and most modern facilities of its kind in the midwest.

The marina has a ship's store, repair shop, and you can see boats for sale displayed in the parking lot and the marina slips. It has swimming, shore fishing and a boat landing. There is a playground for kids and a miniature golf course. There is a sailboat charter service and sailing instruction, for those who want to learn how to sail. There are many sizes of boats to rent. A 25 foot sailboat is the smallest.

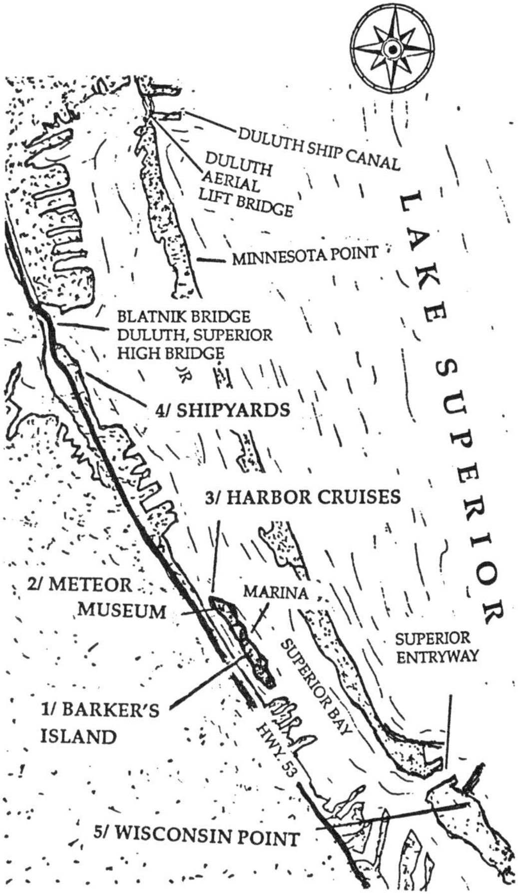

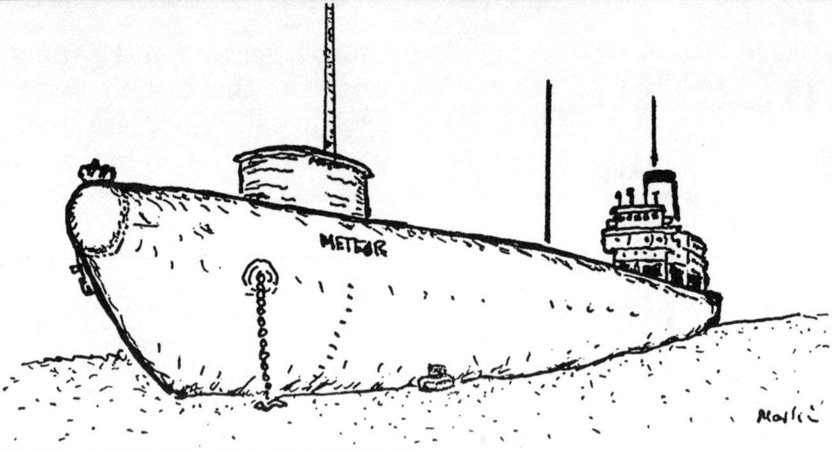

2/ S.S. Meteor Maritime Museum

Whaleback Wharf, Barker's Island
Hwy 2 and 53
(715) 392-5742
Open daily 10 a.m. to 7 p.m. from Memorial Day to mid-August, and to 5 p.m. through Labor Day. Extended hours to 7 p.m. in July. Open weekends to end of October.
Adults $3; children 6-12 yrs and seniors $2.50

This is the last of the old Lake Superior "whaleback" vessels, which were built mainly in Superior in the late 1800's. They were called whalebacks because their rounded decks resembled the tops of whales. The *S.S. Meteor* is now the last remaining whaleback ship.

When you go on board, you can hear the whistle blow and the engines roar. The tour goes through a "real ship" from the deck through captain's and crew quarters to galley and engine room. The whaleback's hold has a museum and displays a collection of pictorial history of whaleback shipping. This interesting tour all over the ship takes about an hour.

Also near the S. S. Meteor is an antique harbor dredge, a lifeboat, and the Seaman's Memorial Statue, dedicated to the 29 members of the crew of the *Edmund Fitzgerald*, a ship that went down on Lake Superior.

Seaman's Statue

3/ Harbor Cruises

Barker's Island
Daily during the season,
May to mid-October.

The Vista Fleet excursion boats sail from Barker's Island throughout the harbor. The modern vessels have narrated cruises and passengers get a first-hand look at the world's largest grain elevators, giant ships anchored in the harbor, and ore docks. For additional details, prices, and route, see *Harbor Cruise (pages 16 and 17).*

4/ SHIPYARDS

South side of the Blatnik High Bridge. Free

You can see usually see many large ships at the Fraser Shipyards, located on Hwy. 2 as you come off the high bridge in Superior. Take a quick glance at the many boats as you drive along the road.

5/ Wisconsin Point

Hwy 2/ 53. Eastern edge of Superior at Moccasin Mike Road. Free

This is Superior's sandy beach and swimming place, just across the ship canal from the Minnesota Point. It's near a lighthouse. You'll probably see a few ships entering or leaving the canal nearby. It's a good place for beach fun, agate picking or searching for souvenir driftwood. Nearby is an old Indian cemetery.

ATTRACTIONS & EVENTS

DULUTH AREA
SUPERIOR AREA

DULUTH ATTRACTIONS

Alworth Planetarium

Located on the University of Minnesota Duluth (UMD) Campus
(218) 726-7129
Free
Public show Wednesday nights at 7 p.m. Show for groups can be arranged.

See the heavens! The evening show usually includes a slide show and a view of the night sky with the star machine as it appears over Duluth. This is a good astronomy experience for children with scientific interests. About an hour in length for the public, a half to three-quarters of an hour for groups. Small groups can be accommodated at the evening show, but call for arrangements.

Biking

Bicycle Touring Trail and biking along the North Shore
Bikeway Maps are available through the Minnesota Department of Transportation
(612) 296-2216
Map costs $3.

Biking is a lot of fun in this area with scenic roads shadowed in north woods' pines.

If you do not have your own bike, bike rental is available in Duluth at Twin Ports Cycler (218-722-0106) or Scenic Cycling, located 1 mile from Carlton (218-384-4180). Bikes also can be rented in a number of places along the North Shore.

Experienced bicyclists rate the Willard Munger State Trail very highly. The trail starts across from the Duluth Zoo, in west Duluth, and continues through Jay Cooke State Park and on to Carlton.

The smooth pavement follows an abandoned railroad bed and has very low grades for easy, traffic-free bike riding. The grades run uphill to Carlton from Duluth.

Round trip bicyclists will probably want to start in Duluth; a one-way trip is easiest if you start in Carlton. It's 14 miles each way, or 28 miles round trip.

The Duluth to Two Harbors bicycle trip (26 miles from Duluth) is also very scenic. The trail starts at Grandma's in Duluth and continues along the Scenic Route Highway north to Two Harbors.

You'll get grand views of Lake Superior. The shoulder of the highway is paved and wide. Bicyclists must negotiate numerous city streets from Grandma's to the north edge of Duluth.

North of Two Harbors, bicycling along Highway 61 is more difficult, due to road shoulder conditions between Two Harbors and Grand Marais (109 miles from Duluth).

The road from Grand Marais to the Canadian border has a road shoulder in better repair. A bicycle trip in this area is enjoyable and the views of the Lake Superior are spectacular.

This can be a long bicycle trip. It involves hills and distances. Be certain you are in good condition.

Cross-country skiing.

Duluth to Grand Marais and practically everywhere else. Information on specific trail conditions is available by calling (800) 657-3700.
Ski Pass required on most public ski trails. Individual $5 per season; $7.50 Husband/Wife

Here is cross-country skiing at its most spectacular. The Minnesota Department of Natural Resources has a cross-country skiing guide which gives information on trails statewide, including level of difficulty, location and what will be encountered on the trail.

There are excellent trails at Grand Portage, Lutsen, Tofte, Schroeder, Silver Bay, Gooseberry Falls, and Two Harbors. More than 150 miles of groomed trails are within 30 minutes of Grand Marais. The North Shore has hundreds of trails and plenty of winter to use them. The Gunflint Trail has an average of 160 days with six inches of snow.

Some skiers find night cross country skiing an adventure. There are three lighted trails in Cook County. The lighted trails are at: Golden Eagle Lodge, lit by lanterns; Bearskin lodge, illuminated by little lights; and Gunflint lodge, illuminated by larger lights.

The Depot

St. Louis County Heritage and Arts Center
Open daily
10 a.m. to 5 p.m. May to mid-October
10-5 Monday to Saturday and 1-5 Sunday, November to April
One admission charge allows admission to all galleries.
Adults $5, Seniors $4, children 6-17 $3
(218) 727-8025

The Depot has a nationally acclaimed collection of antique trains. That's only natural since the Depot originally was a train station. But this favorite tourist attraction also houses four levels of historical and art exhibits.

This includes eight independent heritage and arts organizations, the A.M. Chisholm Museum, the Lake Superior Museum of Transportation, the St. Louis County Historical Society, Duluth Art Institute, The Duluth Ballet, the Duluth Playhouse, Duluth-Superior Symphony Orchestra and Matinee Musicale. There are also two gift shops.

The train museum is a great favorite. Children are allowed to climb on and through many of the trains, cabooses and pullman cars. Children can climb into a railway mail car as well as the cab of the world's largest steam locomotive, whose wheels move. There is a giant railroad rotary snow plow with a video showing how the plow works through mountain snowdrifts. The William Crooks, Minnesota's first steam locomotive, has been beautifully restored. Part of the museum area is a recreated 1910 Duluth street. During the summer season, kids can ride an electric trolley, whose volunteer conductors admit to having even more fun than the kids.

In the Sieur duLhut Room, the St. Louis County Historical Society has a collection of Indian artifacts and a living tree nursery exhibit. The A.M. Chisholm Museum has a walk-in tree where visitors can view local wildlife. The museum also has a touch-and-feel room, which is a favorite for kids. Exhibits change periodically.

Allow 3 to 4 hours if you would like to take in everything. Even if you do, you probably will feel it is worth a return trip.

Duluth News Tribune

424 W 1st St.
Tours are limited to school groups, scouts and other organizations. Free
(218) 723-5281 or (800)-456-8080
To arrange for tours call Jan Chronister direct 723-5262

This is one-hour look at a modern newspaper in operation. Children should be in the 3rd grade or older and be touring with an organization or group. They are taken through all departments and shown how the newspaper is made.

The best time for a visit is when the big presses are running and you can see the newspapers being printed. The tour goes through the production department, newsroom, composing room, and press room.

Call one to two weeks ahead for a reservation. Tours are by prior arrangement only. Times are from 8 a.m. to 4 p.m. The maximum size group allowed is about 20.

Duluth Zoological Gardens

Grand Av. at 72nd Av. West
(218) 624-1502
Open year around, April 1 to Sept. 30, 9 a.m. to 6 p.m. daily. Kids under 4, free; ages 4 to 11, $1.50; over 12 and adults, $3.50.

The Duluth Zoo contains more than 500 animals from around the world. There is a new polar exhibit where you can see polar bears, penguins, lemmings, otters and other polar animals and birds in their natural setting. Children can pet an emu. An indoor exhibit contains crocodiles and exotic fish from the Great Barrier Reef. The Children's Zoo is a favorite where kids can pet the animals. Allow 1 1/2 hours minimum.

Duluth Visitors Bureau

Convention and Visitors Bureau
100 Lake Place Drive
Free

1-800-4 DULUTH or (218) 722-4011

Here's where you can find out just about anything about everything that's happening in Duluth. The bureau provides information on current activities and events in Duluth. It has many brochures and maps and also are very helpful with "Where do I go?" questions.

Enger Tower

Skyline Parkway at 18th Av. West
Free.

This is a five-story, eight-sided stone tower on a hill high atop the city. Climbing to the top of the tower earns the ambitious a panoramic view of the harbor, city and Lake Superior. On a clear day you can see for 30 miles— so far you can actually see the curvature of the earth on the big lake. Kids seem to have unlimited energy to climb the tower stairs. The tower's grounds also contain a Japanese garden. A gazebo at the edge of the bluff overlooks Duluth and the lake.

Fishing

Minnesota fishing license required if age 16 or older.

The best kids' fishing is in the dozens of rivers running into Lake Superior along the shore. Here they can fish for trout— rainbow, brown, and brook using any simple fishing gear, a small hook, a split shot and a worm.

Kids 16 and older need a fishing license and a trout stamp to fish these waters. Both are available from any bait shop or sporting good store in Duluth or along the shore. Kids 15 and younger can fish without a license.

Worms are usually the best bet. Half a nightcrawler works well, too. The best time of the day for fishing in the summer is early morning and evening. When the sun is low and doesn't shine directly on the water, the fish aren't as easily spooked.

The best season is May and June and then again in September. In the mid-summer, the best fishing is on cloudy cool days. Rainy days are good, too.

Kids can expect to catch small fish 6 to 8 inches in length. Older kids who can cast well might try casting a silver or brass spoon directly into Lake Superior, anywhere near the mouths of these rivers: Brule, Cascade, Split Rock, Poplar, Temperance, Baptism, French or Lester. Throughout the year, lake trout (2 to 10 pounds) cruise along the big lake's shoreline, and will hit a spoon at dawn and dusk.

A few of the good spots for stream fishing are near the parking lots on the Lester, Baptism, Caribou, Gooseberry, Temperance and Cascade rivers, either upstream or downstream from Highway 61. On most rivers, the farther inland you go, the better the fishing gets.

It may be important for parents to know that the Department of Natural Resources (DNR) stocks streams in Duluth with catchable trout 6-10 inches long. Call the DNR office at French River Hatchery (218) 723-4881 to find out which rivers were stocked in the current year. Usually Amity Creek and the Lester River are among those stocked.

Glensheen Mansion

3300 London Road
(218) 724-8864 for reservations
(218) 724-8863 for recorded information
Call for current tour times
Adults $6; Children under 6-11, $3; Seniors $5; & children 5 & under free, Family rate $18.

Glensheen is a 22-acre stately mansion located on the shore of Lake Superior. It is listed on the National Register of Historic Places. The Jacobean-revival mansion was built from 1905 to 1908 by Chester & Clara Congdon. Congdon was an attorney, mining entrepreneur, member of the state legislature, and self-made millionaire. The beautiful mansion and grounds, which contain formal gardens, show a family's lifestyle during an elegant period in Duluth's history. There is also an interesting collection of carriages and sleighs in the carriage house. You should allow about 2 hours to tour the house and grounds.

Grain elevators on Connor's Point

Free

The two best places to view grain elevator loading are at the foot of Hammond Ave. or while driving across the Blatnick Bridge. The elevation from the bridge allows a better view, but there is no place on the bridge to stop and look. So look quick.

Grand Slam Adventure World

395 Lake Ave. South
Near Canal Park across the street from the Minnesota Slip Bridge
(218) 722-5667
Sunday-Thursday, 10 a.m. to 11 p.m.
Friday & Saturday, open until midnight. Prices vary

This is a family-oriented entertainment center. It has indoor miniature golf in a castle, batting cages to improve your baseball and softball games, video games, a playground equipment area for young kids, bumper cars, slam dunk, basketball courts, and a snack bar. Bring money.

Hawk Ridge

Between Glenwood Ave. & Lester Park on East Skyline Parkway
August to December is migration time. Free

From this scenic viewpoint on the hill, you can look out over Duluth and the big lake to see thousands of birds, including hawks and other birds of prey, during their fall migration. The migration starts in August and lasts to December. The Minnesota Ornithologic Union schedules "Hawks Weekend" around the third Saturday in September.

A pair of binoculars and a bird book can help in understanding and enjoyment. The fall migration, as seen on Hawk Ridge, draws bird-watchers from around the country.

Jay Cooke State Park

Two miles east of Carlton, MN.
(218) 384-4610
Minnesota State Park fee:
$18 season, $4 per day

Be sure to cross the St. Louis River on the pedestrian suspension bridge. The bridge is a favorite stop for the kids, with good reason. The breath-taking beauty of the park and much of the important geology of the area, are visible from the bridge.

There is interesting geology in Jay Cooke Park. Rock formations consist of slate, graywacke, and red clay. Underground geologic activity caused the slate and graywacke to fold and the rocks protrude, in the St. Louis River bed. Great fun for the kids to climb. In the center of the park the rocky river bed turns abruptly into red clay.

Most of the hiking trails are on the far side of the suspension bridge. Watch out for poison ivy on the hiking trails.

The Willard Munger Bike Trail runs between Jay Cooke Park, Duluth and Carlton. The trail is a good workout for the ambitious biker. A Pioneer Cemetery is also a point of historical interest in the park.

There are a variety of park programs during the summer, conducted by the park naturalist. Check with the park ranger station for the current program.

The park has picnic grounds, an interpretive center, and fishing. There are 80 semi-modern campsites and lots of hiking trails.

Lake Superior & Mississippi Railroad

(218) 624-7549 or 727-8025
Adults $5, Children 12 & under $3,
Seniors $4

Enjoy a 1-1/2 hour ride aboard a vintage train. The train departs Grand Ave. at 71st Ave. West across from the Duluth Zoo. Four trips per weekend on a 12-mile route overlooking the St. Louis River. Beginning in early July, the departure times Saturday & Sunday are 11 a.m. and 2 p.m. This is a shorter and reasonably priced train trip for children. The trip gives spectacular views of the inland scenery.

Duluth Library

520 W. Superior St.
(218) 723-3802
Free

To some people, the library reminds them of an ocean-going ship. At any rate, it's a wonderful place to visit and has a good selection of children's books and videotapes, including popular children's movies.

There is a play area for small children, with toys and games available for use at the library and for checkout. At last count, the library had several hundred toy and game items available. Apple computers are available for use by children who may call ahead and reserve a time slot.

Storytimes are held on Wednesdays, year round. Toddler Time, for children under age two with their parents, is at 10:15 a.m. and Storytime for 3, 4 and 5-year-olds is at 11:15. No registration is required.

The Kaleidoscope series of free programs for children, held each summer, includes musical groups, magicians and jugglers, nature programs featuring animals, storytellers and puppet shows.

Schedules are available in the library. Programs are often held outdoors on the library plaza. Arrive early to park and bring a jacket.

North Shore Scenic Railroad

Lower level Duluth Depot
506 W. Michigan St.
(218) 722-1273 (800) 423-1273
Trains run May 15 to October 17.
They leave promptly, so plan to arrive early.

Here are four terrific train rides along the lake and through the woods of the North Shore. You'll see scenery and views of Lake Superior often not visible from a car. The trip to Two Harbors goes over trout streams, past towns, hidden cabins and north woods forests.

1/ The Laker. Duluth to Two Harbors, a 6-hour trip covering 52 miles of scenic countryside along the North Shore. There is a 2-hour layover at Two Harbors. Leaves Duluth at 10:30 a.m. daily, returning at 4:30 p.m. Adults $15, children $7.50.

2/ Zenith Zephyr. Duluth to the Lester River. The trip is a 1 1/2-hour picturesque trip through Duluth's downtown, waterfront, and residential areas including mansions overlooking Lake Superior. It is a 12-mile trip. Get a unique view of the Duluth Aerial Lift Bridge, lakefront, bayfront and Canal Park. Train leaves at 10 a.m., noon, 2 p.m., and 4 p.m. daily. Adults $8, children $4.

3/ Pizza Train. Duluth to Palmers siding. This 16-mile trip is a 2 1/2-hour round-trip with views of the North Shore. Leaves Duluth at 6:30 p.m. daily. The fee includes pizza and a beverage. Leisurely and with limited narration, with both children's and adult's cars. Adults $16, children $8.

4/ Tom's Trip. Two Harbors to Tom's

Logging Camp. This is a picturesque 1 1/2-hour trip out of Two Harbors along the North Shore to Tom's Logging Camp. You can see how lumberjacks lived and how logs were cut in the old days. Includes a petting zoo. Adults $7, children, $3.50.,

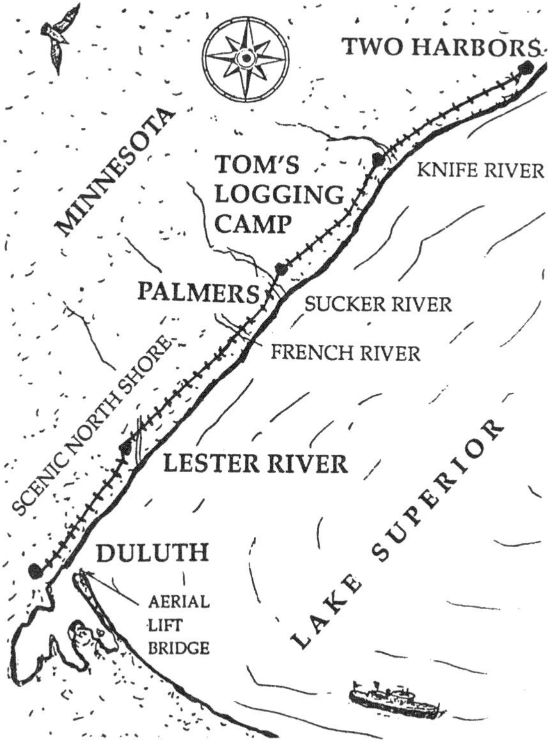

Ore Boat Loading

35th Ave. W. & Superior St. Free

From this observation platform you can see giant ore boats being filled with taconite pellets. Helpful signs explain how the boats are loaded. The ore docks of the Duluth, Mesabe and Iron Range Railway Company extend more than 2,000 feet into the harbor. This is an excellent view of a fascinating activity.

Paper Mill

Lake Superior Paper Industries
100 Central Ave. N.
Memorial Day to Labor Day weekend
Free. Reservations are required.
Summer public tours run Monday, Wednesday and Friday, 9 a.m. , 10:30 a.m., 1 p.m., and 3 p.m. Group tours Tuesday by appointment.
(218) 722-6024 for tickets; (218) 628-5100 Diane M. Laabs for more information. Must be 10 years or older. High heels and open-toed shoes are not permitted.

A mile-long guided tour shows how paper is made. The visit begins with a 10-minute video and an explanation of the paper-making process. Visitors then tour the pulp mill, paper machine, supercalendar, and winders.

It is a good walk, but the education is worth the effort. The mill is high-tech and the visit an educational and interesting one. Older children enjoy this tour the most.

Skyline Drive

Duluth. Free

You can see the city and harbor from the 30-mile long Skyline Drive, in the hills of Duluth at about 600 feet above the water. There are many observation points, with markers, to stop at. Take your camera. You can climb 60-foot-high Enger Tower, 18th Av. on Skyline Parkway, for a panoramic view. It is the highest point in Duluth.

Theatre for the Young

Spirit of North Theatre
600 E. Superior St.
1 p.m. & 3 p.m., when production is underway
Students $2 high school and under, adults $5
(218) 727-5060

Here is a children's theatre not only for kids but put on by kids. Children are directors, designers, and make sets— as well as act. The theatre was founded in 1985 and puts on from one to three productions annually.

Thompson Hill Information Center

South of Duluth, off I-35
Free

You can walk out on the balcony and have a spectacular view of Duluth, Superior and the waterfront. Informative plaques help you orient yourself to your adventure ahead.

This information center is a good place to stop on the way into the city, if you are arriving from the south. You can stretch your legs, see the view, and also have a picnic in several picnic places. Bring binoculars.

Tweed Museum of Art

University of Minnesota, Duluth
Free
(218) 726-8222

The museum is located on the University of Minnesota-Duluth (UMD) campus and has paintings in nine galleries.

This includes collections of American and European paintings. Children who have some interest in art like these galleries.

WDSE Channel 8

1202 E. University Circle
(218) 724-8567. Contact Jodi Hagen.
Free

Kids can see themselves on television, if the equipment is not in use, and learn how a TV station works. This tour of the public TV station is available for groups. You can see the studio, control room and production. It takes about 15 to 30 minutes.

YMCA

301 West 1st St.
(218) 722-4745. Prices vary

The YMCA has a number of classes and activities open to nonmembers as well as members. This includes 15 open swimming times throughout the week and swimming is free to members. The Y has programs in aquatics and gymnastics. Seasonal sports activities, including soccer and wrestling, vary with the time of the year. Call for information.

DULUTH EVENTS

Air Show

Duluth Aviation Expo
July or August in odd-numbered years 1993, 1995, 1997
Adults $5 children $2
Duluth International Airport

The Duluth Aviation Expo is a great time to take a close look at airplanes on the ground and to see them in the skies. There are acrobatic and comedy performers, plus displays of aircraft from the Duluth Air Force Base as well as other military and civilian planes.

The display of planes and activities vary from show to show. If you haven't been to an airshow, this is a good one to see. The show, which runs about three hours, is appreciated most by older children. A suggestion: Take a lawn chair and lunch.

Bayfront Blues Festival

2nd Week in August
Free outdoor festival in Bayfront Park
1-800-4-DULUTH
Six bands daily for three days, 11 a.m. to 9 p.m..

Here's a great festival for the music enthusiast. There are 20 bands on three different stages over the three-day festival. Since a variety of blues music is preformed, older children will enjoy this the most.

Sunday mornings have a gospel breakfast to benefit local charities. There are food concessions. No beverage cans, bottles or coolers are permitted.

Duluth Ballet

(218) 722-2314
The Nutcracker performance: Adults $15; children, students & seniors, $10.
Other performances,
Adults $10; students & seniors, $9; and children, $7.
During the season. Call for performance dates.

The Duluth Ballet is a professional ballet company that presents performances from September to March. The company has a fall performance, the Nutcracker, and a spring performance. The Nutcracker performed in December has a cast of more than 100 dancers.

There's also a ballet school with a variety of programs for children from age 3.

College of St. Scholastica Theatre

1200 Kenwood Ave.
Adults $4; Children $2
(218) 723-6133

Call ahead to find out what's on. The theatre puts on a variety of shows open to the public. Generally, one show per academic quarter is performed. The theatre run is in the last two weeks of the quarter. Curtain time is 8 p.m. evenings and 2 p.m. for the matinees. The two-week run has shows on Friday, Saturday and a Sunday matinee for the first week, and Thursday, Friday and Saturday during the second week.

Grandma's Marathon

Two Harbors to Duluth
Third Saturday in June
Free to spectators. The runners can be viewed along Hwy. 61

About 6,000 runners compete in

Grandma's Marathon each year—and that's a lot of runners. The marathon, one of the outstanding events in the country, is held along the North Shore. Runners begin at Two Harbors and run south beside Lake Superior. They finish in Duluth.

The pre-race activities and events start the Friday before the Marathon in Canal Park. Grandpa's five miler is on Friday and the big race is on Saturday. There is live entertainment during the weekend.

Duluth is very crowded during the event. If you plan to visit Duluth during this event, your family should have lodging reservations months ahead.

John Beargrease Sled Dog Marathon

Duluth to Grand Portage. Third week in January. Free to spectators

The place goes to the dogs—but it's all in great fun. For example, there's a Mutt Race. If your family dog can pull a sled and a child 50 yards, you can qualify for this race. Or you can compete in a kids' ice cube toss. See how many ice cubes you can throw into a container in one minute. There are also contests for the strongest dog and the cutest puppy.

The main activity is the John Beargrease race with sled dogs up and down the North Shore. The event attracts dog sled racers from around the world. It's a thrill to see these old-time racers flying behind their yelping sled dogs and to remember this is how people delivered mail not so long ago when there were no roads along Lake Superior. This is Duluth's celebration to enjoy the winter. Bring warm clothes.

SUPERIOR
ATTRACTIONS & EVENTS

Amnicon Falls State Park, WI.

Summer (715) 398-3000
winter (715) 399-8073
On Hwy. 2 about 8 miles southeast of Superior, WI
Wisconsin Park Permit:
$4 per day, $15 yearly for automobiles with Wisconsin plates.
Non-Wisconsin plates, $6 day, $24 per year.

Here are 825 acres in an untouched setting. The falls dominate in the heart of the park where the river divides and goes over three waterfalls of nearly 30 feet each.

The river split forms an island, which is reached by a covered bridge. This is one of the few covered bridges in the midwest. Take your camera.

The drainage area of the Amnicon River contains the only musky population of Northwestern Wisconsin. Fishing for muskies is done in some of the area lakes.

Unique geology abounds for the rock hound. The park sits on the Douglas Fault, a very old fault line.

The breccia zone is the exact location where the two rock masses moved and is about 12 feet wide. The fault can be seen clearly on the island.

Fairlawn Mansion-Museum

906 E. Second St. (715) 394-5712
Open 9 a.m. to 5 p.m. except holidays.
Adults $4; children 6-13, $1; under 6 free; seniors and 14 to college age $2
Group rates: $ 3.50; seniors & 14 to college $1.50; children 50 cents.

Fairlawn is a 42-room mansion built by Superior's second mayor, the lumber baron Martin Pattison. The entire house is an exhibit. Displays change from time to time Activities have included a children's treasure hunt, movies, railroad display, and various changing displays for kids. There is a large button collection and old clothes from the period. Allow 45 minutes to an hour.

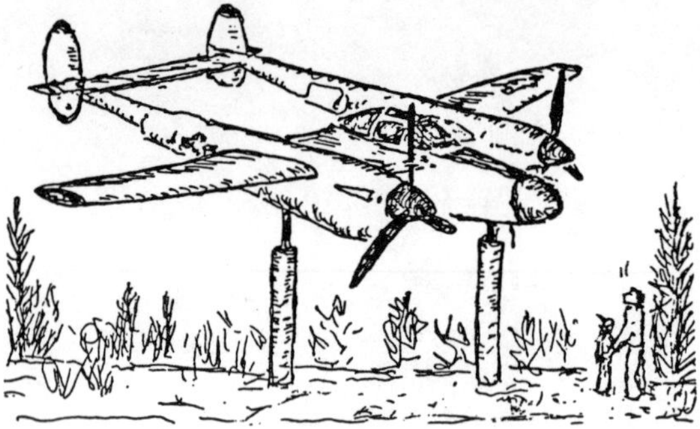

Major Dick Bong Memorial

U.S Hwy. 2, about 20 miles east of Superior. Open summers Monday to Saturday, 9:30 a.m. to 6:00 p.m. Free

Located in Poplar, the memorial features an authentic P-38 fighter plane, one of the few remaining World War II fighter airplanes of its type, and Bong's Congressional Medal of Honor.

This is a monument in memory of a local hero who was known as "Ace of Aces" because he shot down 40 enemy planes during World War II.

Old Firehouse and Police Museum

23rd Ave. East & Fourth St.
(Hwy. 2 & 53)
(715) 2773 or (800) 942-5313
Family $10, Adult $3
and children, $2.50
Open June through August
10 a.m. to 5 p.m. daily

Fire engines and firemen have always been of interest. This is a modest fire museum, but it can be the highlight of the afternoon. The old firehouse is the last of Superior's turn-of-the-century fire stations. Now restored and open to the public, it has antique fire-fighting equipment including a 1906 steam pumper. Tour guides are available. Allow an hour.

Pattison State Park

12 miles south of Superior on Hwy. 35
(715) 399-8073
Wisconsin Park Permit: $4 per day;
$15 yearly for automobiles with
Wisconsin plates; non-Wisconsin
plates, $6 day, $24 year.

Hiking is the best way to see this relatively primitive park. The rapids and the falls on the Black River are its most prominent features and the park is a good place to observe birds and wildlife. Checklists of birds, mammals and cold-blooded creatures are available in the park office. Pattison has 59 campsites, 18 with electric hookups. No sewer or water hookups are available. A dump station is available.

Superior Tourist Information

305 Harbor View Parkway E.
(Hwy. 2 & 53)
(800) 942-5313. Free

At Superior Douglas County Tourist Information, you can find all kinds of information on current activities in Wisconsin. The people are helpful and will answer questions about the area. Ask for brochures and maps.

CARLTON AREA

Whitewater Rafting
of St. Louis River
Superior White Water
950 Chestnut Ave.
Carlton, MN 55718
(218) 384-4637
$29 per person, age 12 and older.
Youth group rates available week days.
Daily trips from May to September

Here is a chance to go whitewater rafting. This is definitely an activity for the older kids. In fact, kids must be at least 12 years of age.

The trip begins in Carlton at Hwy. 210, and takes about 2 1/2 hours. Trained guides accompany the expeditions. This is a chance to shoot whitewater rapids and everyone has an opportunity to use a paddle. It is unusual not to get wet.

Pick a warm day. Wet suits are required in May. Reservations are required.

LAKE SUPERIOR, WOW! HERE ARE SOME FACTS

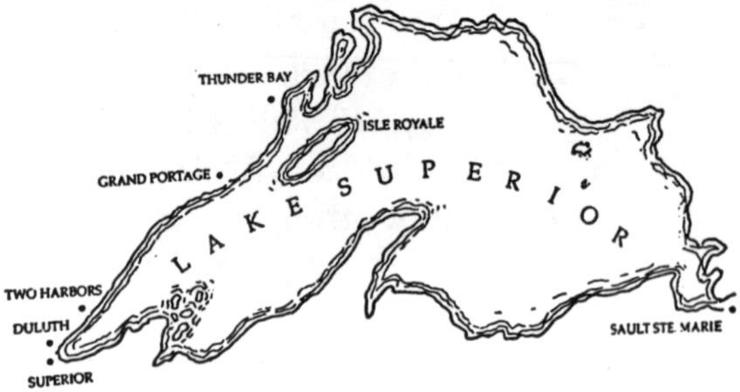

Lake Superior is the largest freshwater lake in the world. Its surface has 31,500 square miles of water.

Lake Superior holds 10 percent of the earth's fresh surface water.

The big lake is 350 miles long and 160 miles wide.

Lake Superior contains three quadrillion gallons. That's enough water to flood Canada, the United States, Mexico and South America with one foot of water.

THE NORTH SHORE

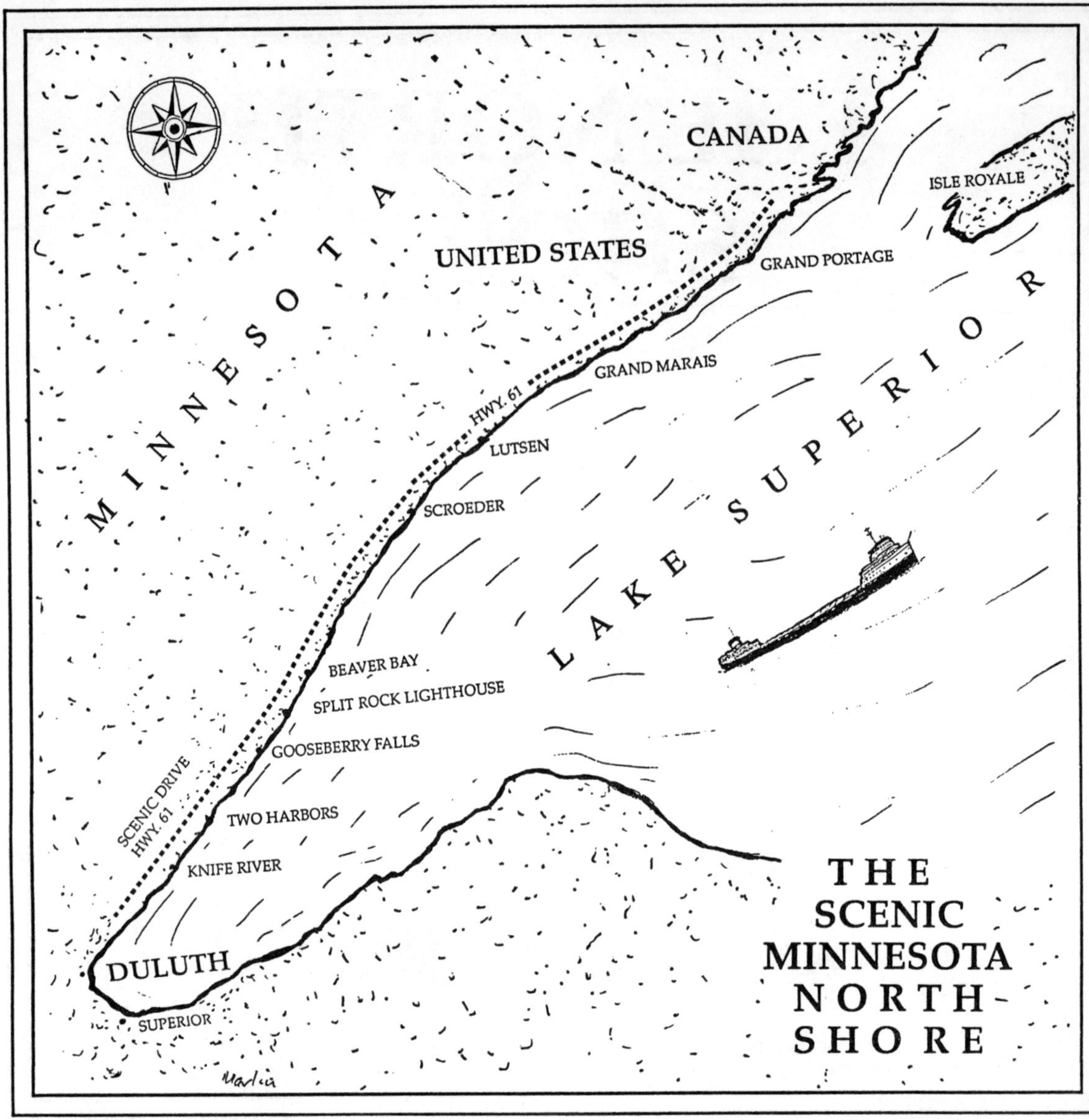
CANADA
UNITED STATES
MINNESOTA
ISLE ROYALE
GRAND PORTAGE
LAKE SUPERIOR
GRAND MARAIS
HWY. 61
LUTSEN
SCROEDER
BEAVER BAY
SPLIT ROCK LIGHTHOUSE
GOOSEBERRY FALLS
SCENIC DRIVE HWY. 61
TWO HARBORS
KNIFE RIVER
DULUTH
SUPERIOR
THE SCENIC MINNESOTA NORTH SHORE

Scenic Drive

Highway 61 from North Duluth to Two Harbors. Free

Take this 28-mile scenic drive along Lake Superior from Duluth to Two Harbors. The scenery and view of the lake are sensational from Duluth and, for that matter, all the way to the Canadian border.

Begin by taking the Scenic North Shore Drive, bypassing the Hwy. 61 expressway to Two Harbors. You'll find the turnoff to the North Shore Drive just north of Duluth along London Road or Superior Street, about a half-mile past 60th street. The scenic road runs close by Lake Superior. There is beautiful shoreline along the way and, usually, boats can be seen gliding along the lake. There are a number of observation lookout points.

The drive is beautiful all year, but especially during the fall color season. Peak color is usually late in September.

Fish Hatchery

Along Hwy. 61 about 12 miles from Duluth. Free
(218) 723-4881
French River fish hatchery tour
8 a.m. to 4:30 p.m. Monday to Friday

It's exciting to see so many fish swimming around. The Minnesota Department of Natural Resources' hatchery has salmon and rainbows. There is a 12-minute video in the visitor's area and computerized games to test your knowledge about fish management.

Visitors can view fingerlings through a viewing window, but are not allowed in that part of the hatchery, due to health considerations for the fish. Yearling raceways are open for viewing and visitors can see the fish being fed.

Spring and fall are the peak activity times for the hatchery. Visitors can see fish being removed from the traps in the morning during the spawning run.

Tours are available for groups of 10 or more. Call ahead to schedule a tour. Visitors are welcome at any time during regular hours.

Sucker River

15 miles northeast of Duluth. Free

The townsite of Montezuma was located here in 1856. The long curved gravel beach to the east was a favorite camping site for early travelers. "Stony Point" on the east end affords protection against Northeast storms.

See the section on fishing, and then try your luck here.

Knife River.

19.5 miles northeast of Duluth. Free

Knife River got its name from an Indian name describing the knife-like rocks in the river. It has charter fishing, a boat launching site, and a full-service marina with 91 slips. Knife River is famous for smoked fish and its agate beach. See the fishing section.

Tom's Logging Camp

5797 North Shore Drive
(218) 525-4120
Open May to October 9 a.m. to 5 p.m.
July 4th to Labor Day 8 a.m. - 7 p.m.
Adults $2; Children age 6-15, $1; under 5 free

Here is an authentic full-scale replica of an early logging camp, complete with bunkhouse, blacksmith shop, cook shanty, water sleigh, and shoeing stall. There is also a fishing museum with original equipment. The self-guided tour includes a trout pond, tame deer, pygmy goats, bunnies, gravity house and nature trail.

The large bunnies have the run of the place. Kids like the pygmy goats, and the tame deer. There is a "gravity house" built at odd angles, and balls appear to roll "up hill". The kids enjoy the distorting mirrors.

The trading post has unique gifts, jewelry, and pottery. The walls are covered with mounted deer, moose, Indian items and other objects. There is no admission charge to the trading post.

Two Harbors

R.J. Houle Information Center
(218) 834-8370 (summer)
Lake County Historical Society
(218) 834-4898
Admission charge for each museum: Adults $1.50; children 9-17 $.75; under 9 free. Family Rate for everyone in the family for all three museums, $10

The Depot Museum, in a railroad building built in 1907 near the waterfront, has exhibits and photographs of the old days of Two Harbors and the North Shore. It is called the Depot because it was once the headquarters of the Duluth and Iron Range Railway. The depot was last used for passengers in 1961. It is now the terminus (end) of the North Shore Scenic Railroad.

Near the Depot are two interesting railroad locomotives, which can be viewed without museum admission. The *Three Spot* was the first engine brought to the area in 1883. Towed to Two Harbors on a scow, it was used on the iron range. There is also a Mallet Engine, one of the largest steam engines ever built.

The **3M/Dwan Museum**, the original office and headquarters of the Minnesota Mining and Manufacturing Co., is where the giant Minnesota corporation first began. John Dwan, a Two Harbors lawyer, was the first corporate secretary for 3M. It is open seven days a week from mid-May through October and is a sandpaper museum, where you can see how sandpaper is made and used.

The **Lighthouse Point & Harbor Museum** is in the only operating lighthouse in Minnesota. Built in 1892, this station is still active and controlled by the Coast Guard. A 45-minute guided tour takes you into the lighthouse, explains how it works, and includes a tour of the turn-of-the century restored

Lightkeeper's House.

Walk out on the pier about a quarter mile and see what Two Harbors looks like from out in the lake. If you take a fishing rod along, you can fish from the pier. You can also get a grand view of the loading docks, where about 10 to 12 million tons of taconite are loaded each year on the giant ore carriers.

On the other side of the entry, to the west of the breakwater, lies a submerged schooner, the Samuel P. Ely. It is one of the older shipwrecks on Lake Superior.

Other things to take in on a driving tour of Two Harbors:

The Sheriff's Residence and Jail, built in 1887, was both home and jail for the county sheriff. The jail was in back of the home.

A great place to look for agates is along Burlington Bay, the other harbor of Two Harbors.

The historic tugboat, *Edna G,* can be viewed from a viewing platform, in Paul VanHoven Park. The platform is across the lakefront park to the west of the Depot Museum about a block. The *Edna G.* was the last steam tug on Lake Superior and had many adventures

The waterfront park is great for gull feeding. Kids can take a loaf of bread and toss pieces into the air. The gulls will wheel by and snatch the bread crumbs in mid-flight. (But don't get too close or try to feed the gulls by hand). Two Harbors also has band concerts in the band shell on summer evenings. The town has the oldest community band in Minnesota. Take a blanket or a lawn chair.

Lake County Visitor Information

(800) 554-2116
(during the summer season).
Free

Helpful people here will send just about any information you want on the Two Harbors area.

Gooseberry Falls

North of Two Harbors
40 miles from Duluth
State Park Permit:
$18 yearly $4 daily.
(218) 834-3855

This is one of the most spectacular falls in Minnesota. The Gooseberry River enters the park at a height of 240 feet above Lake Superior, then cascades over a series of falls and then exits in a series of rapids. You can see it from the highway.

The park has 70 modern campsites, three picnic areas, hiking trails, trout fishing, and programs at the interpretive center. Wildlife and other park programs are arranged by the park staff, check the bulletin board at the interpretive center.

The park has cross country skiing and snowmobile trails for winter enjoyment. The Gooseberry Falls State Park has 1,662 acres and is the second most used state park. Be sure to get a reservation if you are staying.

Rockhounds will appreciate the geology of the area. Some kids have a great time climbing on the sheets of hardened basalt lava flows. But be careful.

There are five waterfalls on the Gooseberry river within the park. Two are easily accessible with a short walk from Hwy. 61.

Allow about an hour for just looking around.

Split Rock Lighthouse

19 miles north of Two Harbors on Hwy. 61.
(46 miles north of Duluth)
State Park Permit Season $18 daily $4
$3 admission charge to lighthouse.
Open all year
History Center 9 to 5 p.m.
Park office 8 a.m.- 10 p.m.
State Park Historic Site 226-4372 or (218) 226-3065

Split Rock Lighthouse is probably the most photographed site on Lake Superior. It was erected in 1910 after a November 1905 storm sank six ships along the North Shore, three within 12 miles of the site. The part of Lake Superior's rugged shore it guards has been referred to as the "most dangerous piece of water in the world."

You can climb to the lighthouse, high atop a 130-foot cliff, and look far over Lake Superior's gusty waters. On a clear day, you can see many ships and far in the distance, Wisconsin.

The lighthouse and history center comprise a 25-acre historic site. Entry fee is $3 for adults and $1 for children 6-15. Admission to the historic site includes a complimentary pass into Split Rock State Park for the day. The history center presents some of the history of the lighthouse, shipwrecks and commercial fishing on Lake Superior.

Surrounding the lighthouse is the 1,872-acre state park. If you want to camp at this park, you pay the park fee. If you also want to see the lighthouse, you pay an additional $3 fee. There are twenty campsites, each with a table and fire ring located along shore of Lake Superior. The park has modern sanitation, showers, visitors center, historic site, six miles of hiking trails, fishing and picnicking. You can hike the trails down to Lake Superior. Allow about an hour.

Beaver Bay

Five miles north of Split Rock Lighthouse (50 miles northeast of Duluth). Free

A totem pole in Beaver Bay marks the Indian cemetery that dates from 1865. John Beargrease is buried here. He was the colorful pioneer North Shore mailman who delivered mail from 1879 to 1899 by dogsled in the winter. That's because in the early days there was no highway along the North Shore—only a trail through the woods. The John Beargrease dogsled marathon is named for him.

The cemetery is located two blocks north of the Holiday station, on the west side of the street.

Tettegouche State Park

(218) 226-3539
(59 miles northeast of Duluth)
State Park Permit:
Season $18, daily $4

Tettegouche is a good hiking park. One trail leads to the top of Mt. Baldy, 1,000 feet above Lake Superior. On a clear day you can see the Apostle Islands. The trail system is 23 miles. The park has six inland lakes. All have good fishing. Shovel Point on Lake Superior is the most prominent geographic feature in the park. The Baptism River flows through the park. It has the highest waterfalls inside the state boundaries. It's a three-fourths mile walk to the falls. This is an 8,960-acre state park with a rest area, public recreation, information station, picnic areas, fishing, and 34 semi-modern campsites.

Cross River Wayside

Schroeder
(80 miles northeast of Duluth). Free

The river was named in honor of Father Baraga, a pioneer priest who in 1846 crossed from the Wisconsin shore of Lake Superior with an Indian paddler. They survived a terrific storm and giant waves in a birch-bark canoe.

He put up a cross in gratitude for his escape. This cross marked the place where he stepped onto land. Later, a stone cross replaced the original wooden one.

Father Baraga, a historical hero of Lake Superior and known as "The Snowshoe Priest," also wrote an Ojibwa dictionary and translated the Bible into Ojibwa.

The falls can be seen from the Hwy. 61 bridge. The site where the cross was placed is not on state property. It can be found by following the signs from the wayside park on Hwy. 61.

Carlton Peak and Tofte Ranger Station

83 miles northeast of Duluth
Bicycle maps are available for bike touring.

This is the highest peak on the North Shore. It stands 927 feet above the lake level. There are trails for wonderful hiking trips. Travel 1.5 miles up Forest Service Road 343 and look northeast to see the peak.

The peak is composed of anorthrosite —a rare volcanic product mostly consisting of labradorite. It is identified by its transparent green color. You can hike to see it from the trailhead. It's about two miles up the Sawbill Trail. You can also follow the hiking trail which crosses the Sawbill Trail and continue to Temperance River State Park. The trail comes out at the gorge of the Temperance River. You can follow the trail down to Hwy. 61. This is not a difficult hiking trail and the views are spectacular.

Feed the gulls

Free. Many locations

Take along a loaf of bread and tear it into small bits and watch the action when you toss it into the air. Once the gulls start coming, there will be plenty of excitement. Some younger children find this simple activity to be one of the highlights on a visit to the North Shore.

If you are planning ahead, and want to lay in your bread supply inexpensively, Master Bakery has two thrift stores: 3902 E. Hwy. 2 in Superior, and 217 N, 59th Ave. W. in Duluth. You can buy days old bread here—and the gulls don't know the difference.

Temperance River

West of Tofte
(84 miles northeast of Duluth)
State Park Permit, Season $18, daily $4
(218) 663-7476

The Temperance River drops 162 feet in a series of cascades. There are large potholes and cauldrons in the spectacular rocky gorge of the river bed. The river got its name because there is no "bar" at the mouth, as it enters Lake Superior. This is a good fishing spot. If the fish aren't hungry, the gulls always seem to be. There are 50 semi-modern campsites, a fishing stream, picnic grounds, and six miles of hiking trails.

Sawbill Trail

(83 miles northeast of Duluth). Free

This 23-mile trail is a key entry point into the Boundary Waters Canoe Area. Plenty of wildness country, good fishing and lumber camps along the trail.

Alpine Slide

Eagle Mountain at Lutsen
1 1/2 miles off Hwy. 61 at Lutsen
(90 miles northeast of Duluth)
(218) 663-7281
$3.75 all ages. Open mid-May to Mid-October

Take an exciting ride down a 2,200-foot track through the forest on the Alpine Slide. You begin with a chairlift to the summit of Eagle Mountain. Then either take the Alpine Slide down or continue with the chairlift. This has to be rated as one of the really novel activities along the North Shore. Small children often ride well on the Alpine slide on the lap of an adult.

Moose Mountain Gondola

Lutsen 1 1/2 miles off Hwy. 61 at Lutsen.
Open all year
(218) 663-7281
Adults $7.75; Seniors $6.75; Children $4.75; under 6 free with an adult.

This is the midwest's only gondola. It has four-person cars on a mile-long ride. An enclosed car gives access to 800-foot-high Moose Mountain, one of the highest spots on the North Shore. The ride lasts eight minutes over the forests and the Poplar River. It is a great way to view the scenery. From the top you can see almost 100 miles on a clear day. During the fall color season it is an especially lovely view.

Cascade River State Park

Nine miles southwest of Grand Marais
(100 miles northeast of Duluth)
(218) 387-1543
Fees: Annual $18, Daily $4
Hiking trails, picnic grounds.

The Cascade River flows through a twisting rocky gorge in a series of frothing rapids. The river drops some 225 feet over a distance of one mile, to where it flows into Lake Superior.

The park borders the North Shore for about 12 miles and covers 2,800 acres. The panorama is great for camping.

There are fishing opportunities for stream angling and shore fishing on Lake Superior. Some of the trails go up into the Sawtooth Mountains from the park. Fishing and hiking opportunities are the most important activities in this park.

Artist's Point

Grand Marais
(109 miles northeast of Duluth). Free

Walk from the Coast Guard station out onto this peninsula, which juts into Lake Superior. Choose a nice day. Climbing on the rocks is fun for the kids and a breath-taking view for the adults. It's a relatively easy hike.

The Book Station

12th Ave. W.
Grand Marais (218) 387-2153

The store has a wonderful collection of children's books, Ojibwa culture books and nature books. It also has a free brochure that reviews books for children. The store also carries art supplies, arts and crafts from local artists, bead and related beadcraft supplies and how-to books on bead craft.

North Shore Music Series

Grand Marais
(218) 663-7879.
Tickets $8 at the door

The North Shore Music Association sponsors Saturday concerts throughout the summer. The concerts are usually at 8 p.m. at various locations throughout the county.

Recommended for older children, but enjoyment depends on the music preformed. Days may vary, and some concerts are aimed at younger children. Call for a schedule. Tickets are available at the door.

Cook County Fair

Grand Marais
Free

Cook county has the smallest population of any county in Minnesota. This is a small county fair. It is held the first week in August. There are excellent 4H displays.

Grand Marais Art Colony

(218) 387-2737
Older children. Prices vary

The Grand Marais Art Colony, located in a former Catholic Church, operates throughout the summer. There are art exhibits and workshops on art and poetry. The purpose of the workshops is to provide a serious art experience to the visual artist.

Gunflint Trail

Grand Marais. Free

The Gunflint Trail is a very scenic drive that begins here and winds 63 miles north through the Superior National Forest. It ends at the Boundary Waters Canoe Area. The trail rises about 1,000 feet in the first three miles. There are plenty of trees, birds, wild flowers and wildlife to look at.

Canoeing, fishing, lodging, and camp grounds are found along the trail. Check with the Grand Marais Visitor Information Center for information on specific activities and prices. The Visitor Center's number is 1-800-622-4014

Also check with them on the feeding times and locations of the black bears. These can be seen at various places, notably the local trash dump. Get details on where to go and what to do. Staying in your car, windows up and doors locked, to see wild bears rummaging about can be a highlight of the trip.

Hedstroms's Lumber Mill

Grand Marais
(218) 387-1750 U.S. Forest Service
(218) 387-1745 (Mill number)
Memorial Day to Labor Day, Tuesday and Thursdays
arranged through the Forest Service
On Maple Hill North of Grand Marais. Free
2 miles out of town west on Hwy. 61

Call the Forest Service for mill tours. The tour is available with reservations but the tours fill up quickly. It's a good idea to plan in advance if you want to take the tour. A brochure for a self-guided driving tour of the forest areas is available from the Forest Service. It shows the types and ages of forests and their regeneration after fire or harvest.

This popular tour shows how a modern sawmill makes lumber for homes and other uses. The tour shows the logs' journey through the mill, including bark stripping operations, cutting and storage of lumber.

The tour of the mill takes about half hour. The tour is recommended for 8 and up, but younger children are welcome. The catwalk view of the operations is a delight for the older children but some younger ones are apprehensive. The close-up view of cutting operations is noisy.

Visitors meet at the Grand Marais library to watch a short film and then go to the mill. Call for arrangements of groups.

Grand Marais Public Library

1st St. and West 2nd Ave.
(218) 387-1140
Monday - Friday, 10 a.m. to 5 p.m., Wednesday, 10 a.m. to 8 p.m.; Saturday, 10 a.m. to 2 p.m.

You do not need to be a Grand Marais resident to use the library. Any current Minnesota library card, or a $5 fee for non-state residents, allows patrons to check out books.

The library has children's books, a toy collection, videos, computers, as well as a summer reading program.

Lions Club Fisherman's Picnic

Grand Marais
Grand Marais Visitor Information Center 1-800-622-4014. Most events are free

This is a four-day festive event that is held during the first week of August.

There are rock skipping contests, loon calling contests, and a fireworks Saturday night. Friday night is the Miss North Shore queen contest. The fisherman's picnic parade is Sunday afternoon. Try a fishburger. The stand is open all four days. Merchants have a crazy-day sale. A fishing contest goes on during the picnic, with the weigh-in at Hardware Hank's. There are golf and tennis tournaments during the picnic.

The Loafer Bakery

411 W. Hwy. 61, at the western edge of downtown

The Loafer has some of the best cinnamon caramel rolls in the state of Minnesota. There are lots of other good things to eat too!

Miniature Golf

Grand Marais & Lutsen Ski Area. Prices vary

A fun thing to do is to play miniature golf. Check tourist information at Grand Marais or Lutsen information for costs and directions.

Paddleboating

Grand Marais, at the western edge of the harbor.
Paddleboat rental $6 per half hour; $10 per hour

The boats seat two adults and one

child. It is an opportunity to get out on the water and paddle around the harbor during good weather. Looking down into the depth of this Lake Superior harbor is fascinating. You can view the bottom to a considerable depth. Try this on a quiet day. There are also sailboats for rent for the more experienced sailors.

Rock Picking

Grand Marais and the North Shore.
Free

Agates, thomsonites and other rocks are waiting to be collected along the shore of Lake Superior. A handbook on rocks can make this more enjoyable for youngsters. This is a good way to teach a little geology and make it fun. Thomsonites can be found in abundance on the beach at the wayside park four miles west of Grand Marais. There are no toilet facilities at this wayside park, so plan accordingly. If you don't find any rocks worth keeping, you can always skip them on the water.

Saw Tooth Elementary School

Grand Marais
Call community education (218) 387-2000 for further information.

The school has a children's playground and a summer activities program for K through 12. It is open to everyone in this age group. If you are staying in the Grand Marais area, check for programs and times.

Swimming Pool

Grand Marais
Summer Hours: Monday - Friday 10:30 a.m. to 1 p.m.. Adult Swim; Friday open swim, 1 to 11 p.m.
Sunday - Saturday 1 a.m. to 9 p.m.
(218) 387-1275
Adult $4 ; 7-17 $2.50; 0-6 $1.25

Located at the Grand Marais recreation area, at the eastern edge of the trailer park, the swimming pool also includes a sauna and hot whirlpool.

Open all year. The indoor, heated pool is the best place to swim in Grand Marais.

The U.S. Forest Service

Grand Marais
(218) 387-1750
Hwy. 61 & the Gunflint trail.
Open approximately June 15th through Labor Day. Free

The Forest Service has a naturalist program in Grand Marais. The program includes field trips for children, as well as many other activities about the outdoors.

A schedule of current events is available at the Forest Service Station.

The Forest Service building has interesting animal displays, posters as well as much area information.

Magney State Park

14 miles northeast of Grand Marais on Hwy. 61.
(124 miles northeast of Duluth)
(218) 387-2929
Park permit annual $18, daily $4
Park office open until dark on summer nights.

Judge C.R. Magney State Park has 4,514 acres of heavily forested park for hiking, fishing, bird watching, and picnicking. Miles of hiking trails, ski trails and the Brule River wind their way through the park. This is a pretty spot and a good place to see what a real wilderness looks like. There are waterfalls and boiling rapids. The "Devil's Kettle," famous along the North Shore, is located in the park. Water comes over Pothole Falls and disappears underground into a rock cauldron. It is a mystery because no one knows where the water reenters the river. The trail back to the Devil's Kettle is about 1 1/2 miles and climbs up and down. It can be a challenge to very young children.

The Witch Tree

**On the shore near
Grand Portage. Free**

The legendary Witch tree is rooted on lichen-covered rock overlooking Lake Superior. Weather and wind have twisted and gnarled the "Witch Tree" into a spiral. This tree is 400 years old and is one of the oldest trees in the state. Voyageurs offered tobacco at the base of the tree for a safe journey across the dangerous water. The site is of spiritual significance to Indians. Ask at Grand Portage Lodge for directions. 1-800-232-1384

Historic Fort

**Grand Portage National Monument
41 miles north of Grand Marais,
near the Canadian border
(218) 387-2788
Information center open
8 a.m. to 5 p.m.
Adults $1; seniors and under 17 free
Max $3 per car.**

This is the first white settlement in Minnesota. Established in 1731, it was the center of the fur trade 260 years ago. The old fur fort was the end of the historic voyageurs' long paddle and portage from New France along a river and lake highway that included Lake Superior.

Here trade goods were transferred from large lake canoes and fur pelts were loaded for the return voyage. There is a Museum of History of the Voyageurs, a Northwest Fur Company Trading Post and living history and cultural demonstrations. The stockade, great hall, kitchen, warehouse and other reproductions recreate the settlement of 200 years ago. Usually, something is being cooked over the open hearth, and if you are lucky you will be allowed to taste.

An interesting 10-minute video of the history of the trading post is shown on request. Guides in colorful attire will tell you about the fur trade days. In August, the fort re-enacts the annual gathering of voyageurs and Indians. This includes events such as canoe racing, ax throwing, musket firing demonstrations and starting a fire without matches.

The "High Falls" on the Pigeon River can be seen best from the Canadian side of the river. Admission is charged to view the falls, since the site is on private property.

There is a scenic outlook. A short hike, of about 3/4 mile up to Mt. Josephine, provides a thrilling view of Lake Superior and Canada. The hike is steep and arduous; very small children may have difficulty.

St. Johns Catholic Church at Grand Portage is the oldest Catholic Church in Minnesota. Originally an Indian mission, the log structure was built in 1865 and still has an active congregation.

Grand Portage is the closest point in Minnesota to Isle Royale National Park, which is both the most remote park in the U.S. and the nation's least visited. From the Grand Portage dock, in the shadows of the old fur fort, you can take a ferry to this island, 22 miles from shore. It can be a very nice lake cruise, providing the lake cooperates. You can go over, see a little of this remote and mysterious island, and come back over in the same day. Trips leave in the morning.

The Grand Portage Elementary School, built in 1928, is one of the very few remaining log schoolhouses in the country.

The second weekend in August the Chippewa Indians hold a Rendezvous and Pow Wow, with tribal dancing and costumes.

MY SUPERIOR TRIP PLANNER

What to do & where to go for a fun two-day weekend

A two-day planner for a fun weekend visit

Background

This is an area with a lot of things to see and do. However, you may not have enough time to do them all. In fact, many kids and their families are in the area for just a weekend.

That's why this chapter is for you. It can help you, step by step, find your way to some of the most interesting and fun things to do.

Each day is divided into parts: morning, noon, afternoon, and late afternoon and early evening. That is so you can have some idea of the time you can spend at each attraction or event. If you spend more time than you planned, don't worry. The idea is to have fun. You may have to choose which things you'd rather do, though.

You can make up your own schedule, too. Just look at the pages after this section, "My list of things to see and do on my next visit." Here you can write down what you want to see and do. Ask your adult companions for their ideas.

Sometimes the place you want to visit may have made changes. It is a good idea for you or a grownup to call and check times and other important things.

Use your own best judgment and listen to your parents. The things we have talked about are what kids can do when parents are around to help them. Don't do anything you wouldn't do at home.

The things we have picked are planned for energetic kids and their adult companions, who may not have all the energy that kids have. Often that will be okay.

For example, kids may love to run along a beach or a walkway.

Adults can enjoy sitting on the beach nearby and watching. They should be close enough to see you, though.

Some other notes:

- It is a good idea to make reservations for lodging in advance, especially on summer weekends.

- Many of the activities north of Duluth are outdoor. They are things like hiking, camping, rock gathering, and fishing. If you are not experienced, do some homework before starting out. It will make the experience more enjoyable and successful.

- Check your library or book store. A book on birds, trees, or a guide to flowers or a rock guide and other nature books can make the outdoors much more interesting.

- And, last, though we've taken a lot of care to get times and hours right, do call ahead. Days, events, and hours do change.

Day 1

A two-day weekend trip will give you a quick look at this exciting area. We've arranged a tour for you to follow that will give you some good ideas for fun. You won't be able to do everything, and to even try would be a mistake. You will, however, get to do what some kids tell us is the most fun in just a short time.

Highlights: The water, boats, trains, and a swim.

Special things to bring: A loaf of old bread, swimming suit, roller blades or roller skates, shovel and pail. Also a light coat or sweater because it gets chilly here.

Morning

Let's say you and your family just drove up to Duluth. And, boy, are you ready to do something fun!

Hey, a really great place to begin is to head right for the water. Canal Park, beside the waterfront and the Marine Museum, is the place to go. (You can read about this area on pages 20-21). After you park your car, walk over to the ship canal. The big bridge over to your right is the famous Duluth Aerial Lift Bridge (read page 13).

Look out over the water. You probably will be able to see many boats coming and going. From time to time, you will hear a lot of noise. That will be the Aerial Lift Bridge, signalling that it is about to go up. A ship will be coming through. Wait and watch. It will pass through so close you'll get a great view of it. It will look as if you can almost reach out and touch it.

Now, take a hike. Walk out onto the pier leading out from Canal Park.

It's about 1,000 feet, or so, into famous Lake Superior. As you walk along, you will get a feel for the lake's cold water and fresh breezes. At the end of the pier is a lighthouse. Look out over the water for a while and see all the boats. Then come on back.

Now that you've moved around somewhat, it's time to feed the gulls (read page 22). Get your loaf of old bread and head for the grass on Canal Park. Tear off a chunk of bread, toss it high into the air and stand back.

Your friends, the gulls, have been watching you. And when you toss the bread into the air, they will fly in, wheeling and capering, and catch the chunk. What fun! Pretty soon there will be a lot of them flying around. It's important to remember that gulls are wild creatures. Don't try to touch the gulls. Or try to feed the gulls by hand. Just toss the bread in the air (with your adults nearby) and stand back.

Once your bread is gone, it's time to do something new. You're probably feeling pretty good right now. Go back to the car and get your roller blades or roller skates and try out the Lakewalk boardwalk (page 18).

There are actually two boardwalks, actually. One is for skaters, roller bladers, and bicyclists. You can now whiz along the waterfront, having a great time in the fresh air.If you don't have roller blades or skates, just walk or skip along the other boardwalk.

From time to time you will go by a lakefront marker. They are signs with some pictures or words on them. They point out interesting things about the lake, like where a sunken ship lies underneath the water. Go about a mile and then turn around and come back.

Mid-morning

While you're here, and feeling a little more like looking around, take a visit inside the Marine Museum. That's the building right alongside Canal Park. In front is an old lifeboat that used to save lives on Lake Superior. Stop for a quick look.

Now go inside. Take a look on the second floor at all the ship models. These are models of the kinds of ships that once were on Lake Superior. You can see how ships have changed, from sailing to giant 1,000 foot-long ore boats.

Look at the old-fashioned diving suit with a big copper helmet. Can you imagine putting on the helmet and the suit with all the weights on it? And then going down into Lake Superior? Take a look at what modern divers are bringing up from the lake bottoms. There are some displays here.

Now go to the pilot house. It's actually part of an old Superior boat. You can walk right in and stand where the Captain stood. You can try turning the beautiful wooden wheel.

As you look out from your captain's post over the lake, keep listening to the radio. A voice will tell you about what boats will be coming in the canal below. You can then go over to the window and look through one of the telescopes!

Noon

Time for lunch. Your family may have brought a picnic lunch. The lawn at Canal Park is a great place to enjoy it. Or else there are a number of good places to eat nearby, including fast-food restaurants and specialty restaurants.

Early Afternoon

Time for a stroll. Walk up the street to the west to the Minnesota Slip Lift Bridge (read about it on page 28).

It's a tiny, tiny little bridge that is a pedestrian lift footbridge. That means it lifts up to let boats in and out. As you walk over it you can look at the boats nearby.

Now you will see, to your right, one of the biggest boats you'll ever be on. This is the *S.S. William A. Irvin* (read pages 23-25). There is an admission charge to get on board (see the section on Ore Boat Tour) but you get to go all over this boat. This is really a lot of fun. Remember that this was once a working ore boat that sailed all over the lake. It was known as "The pride of the silver stackers." As you stand in the wheelhouse, you can image what it is like to pilot such a giant ship around the harbor. Or, if your imagination is really lively, what it would be like to be in a storm.

Mid-afternoon

By now if it is a sunny day, and the summer wind is off the lake, it's time to head back to the car and drive across the Aerial Lift Bridge onto the Minnesota Point (read page 29). You go all the way to the end where there is a park. You can park your car, walk over the sand dunes, and you'll see miles of sandy beach.

If it is a warm summer day, you may want to go into the water's edge with your adults. The lake often is very cold, but as kids have discovered, the sun on the shallow waters near shore warms up the water just great. Sometimes, to nearly 80 degrees! It is a nice sandy beach that seems to go out gradually, so you can have fun wading, playing in the water, or paddling around. Bring your shovel & pail. You can have a great time building sand castles.

Late afternoon, early evening

Have something to eat. And now, a final treat. As the afternoon fades, you are about to take a harbor cruise. Go to the Vista Fleet dock, on Harbor Drive (read pages 16-17). That's near that little footbridge and the S.S. William A. Irvin. The ships sail every two hours (summer schedule) and your adults should check final sailing time. But it's usually at 7:30 p.m. during the season.Pay your fee and go on board. As the sun sets you will motor out onto Lake Superior. See how the Aerial Lift Bridge goes up for you? Now, as the bow reaches out past the canal into the open waters of the world's largest freshwater lake, feel how the motion of the ship changes.

Then you'll go back again into the harbor. The sun is going down now, bathing the harbor and the waterfront in a golden light. Enjoy being on the water. Listen to your guide tell you about the things and places you can see from the boat. Then, return to your room. Rest well.

Day 2

Highlights: A make-believe castle, climbing, the water, an old boat, and a special train.

What to bring: wear clothing you can play in. Also a light coat or sweater.

Morning

Time to visit a castle. One that you can play on. Actually, there's a dragon, too. But you'll find out. Head down to the waterfront and the Playfront Park (read page 27). It's located on Harbor Drive, just about a block west of the big ore boat you were on. Enter the castle. You can play all around and find the dragon.

Mid-morning

Now it's time to see a train. Or rather, a lot of trains. You will find a big collection of trains of all kinds in The Depot. This place is called The Depot because that it was it once was: Duluth's train station (page 38).

Go downstairs to the train museum. You can climb on and through many of the trains. Look for the oldest train, the William Crooks. And look for the world's largest steam locomotive, whose wheels move. Look also for the giant railroad snow plow, with a videotape showing how the plow works through really big snowdrifts.

When you are finished with the trains, take a ride on an electric trolley. This is a lot of fun. Notice that part of the museum is sort of old fashioned. That is because part of it is built like Duluth used to be in 1910. Look in the store windows. But there is a lot more to do at the Depot. Go upstairs to look at the Historical Society's collection of Indian artifacts. Go over to the A. M. Chisholm Museum where you can walk in a tree and see wildlife. Also, try the touch-and-feel room.

Noon.

Lunchtime. Head off for an island today. You go high up over the Duluth Superior high bridge (look at all the ships below) and then turn off for Barker's Island in the harbor, located in Superior, Wisconsin. You can eat at one of the fast food restaurants or enjoy a picnic lunch here.

Afternoon

You are going inside a whaleback now. This is the S. S. Meteor Maritime Museum (page 32), the last of the old Lake Superior "whaleback" vessels. These special ships were built here in the late 1800's and were called whalebacks because the tops of the ships resembled tops of whales. The idea was that in storms the big waves would roll right over the decks. Pay your entry fee, and go on board. This wonderful old ship was built in 1896 and is listed in the National Register of Historical Sites. It is a lot older than the Irvin that you were on board yesterday.

You can get a feel of what an old ship was like. In a guided tour, you go all the way through the ship, from the engine room up to the wheelhouse. Inside, also, is a display with pictures.

Walk around the Whaleback Wharf area. Play miniature golf in the 18-hole miniature golf course. Use the playground.

Then head off for an unusual supper.

Late afternoon

Be on time, for the Pizza Train leaves promptly at 6:30 p.m. daily during the season. You go back to the Depot and head for the lower level. Your Pizza Train (page 46) leaves Duluth heading along the North Shore in a 2 1/2-hour round trip ride. You get pizza and a beverage, and best of all, there are both children's and adult cars. You come back tired but happy.

This ends your busy two-day weekend in Duluth and Superior. You have done only a few of the 99 things to see and do in this area. But that's fine. It leaves some more things for you and your family to do on your next visit.

My list of things to see & do on my next trip

Write below your own list of things you want to see and do on your next trip. After each, write how long you want to spend at each one.

INDEX

Duluth

Superior

Carlton

The North Shore